The Michigan
Motor Vehicle
ACCIDENT
Book

And How to Avoid 7 Critical Insurance Claim Mistakes

BARBERI LAW

2305 Hawthorn Drive, Ste C,
Mt. Pleasant, MI 48858

1-800-336-3423

www.barberilawfirm.com

Printed in the United States of America.

ISBN: 978-1-59571-949-2
Library of Congress Control Number: 2013918908
$18.95

Designed and published by

Word Association Publishers
205 Fifth Avenue
Tarentum, Pennsylvania 15084

www.wordassociation.com
1.800.827.7903

A Consumer Guide to Help Michigan Motor Vehicle Accide

Victims Recover Compensation for their Injuries and Losses

The Michigan
Motor Vehicle
ACCIDENT
Book

And How to Avoid 7 Critical Insurance Claim Mistakes

Michigan residents:

If you have been injured in an auto, truck, or motorcycle-motor vehicle accident don't get injured twice—the second time by an insurance company!

Do I need to hire an attorney to settle my claim?

Attorney Joseph T. Barberi

nt

Table of Contents

Introduction

This book has been written to explain how Michigan's No-Fault Law works and to make it easier for Michigan consumers to obtain the benefits they are entitled to receive as a result of paying insurance premiums, or as a result of being injured by a motor vehicle in or outside of the State of Michigan. In some cases, individuals within the State of Michigan who don't have any motor vehicle insurance are injured by someone operating a motor vehicle. This can happen when a pedestrian, motorcycle rider, or occupant of someone else's motor vehicle is injured. Michigan's No-Fault Law provides coverage to injured individuals even though they may not have their own insurance or even own a motor vehicle—think for example of children. Michigan has one of the best thought-out insurance coverage programs in the nation, and this author is hopeful that Michigan's No-Fault Law, as currently written, will not dramatically change in the future.

This book is divided into eight sections. The **first section** provides background information on Michigan's No-Fault Law. The **second section** focuses on initial considerations after a motor vehicle accident and becoming familiar with "terms of art" used by those who regularly process No-Fault claims. The **third section** focuses on how you obtain PIP benefits. The **fourth section** focuses on how individuals can be compensated for serious injuries, a serious permanent disfigurement, or for a death caused by an at-fault driver of a motor vehicle. The **fifth section** deals with hiring an attorney to help you settle your first or third party claim. The **sixth section** deals with seven things that can harm your motor vehicle case. The **seventh section** provides answers to frequently asked questions about Michigan's No-Fault Act and actions to take to protect your rights to receive compensation and benefits. The **eighth section** discusses why hiring a central and northern Michigan motor vehicle accident attorney might be best for you.

It is hoped that by reading this book, Michigan consumers will become informed and assisted in obtaining compensation for injuries, a serious permanent disfigurement, or a death which occurred as a result of a motor vehicle accident.

Overview of Michigan's No-Fault Law

History and Rational

Prior to October 1, 1973, the date that Michigan's No-Fault Insurance Act became law, injured persons in motor vehicle accidents were able to sue the driver of the vehicle responsible for their accident for all of the injuries and damages they received. However, if the injured party was found to have contributed to the accident in even the slightest he or she was barred from *any* recovery. This harsh rule prevented some seriously injured victims of motor vehicle accidents from receiving any compensation.

Many injured persons were required to sue the at-fault driver to recover any benefits. As a result, injured persons often faced lengthy delays in receiving compensation for their lost wages and medical expenses. Injured parties were often forced to take significantly less compensation than they might otherwise have been entitled to receive. If they were off work and having bill collectors knocking at their doors, some money was better than none! And medical providers were also often left to wonder when, and if, they would receive payment for their treatment of the injured party.

After October 1, 1973 the No-Fault Insurance Act gave individuals immediate access to medical treatment without having to wait for the at-fault driver's insurance company to adjust their claim. Additionally, the No-Fault Act provided that the injured party's own insurance company would compensate for lost wages for up to three years after the motor vehicle accident. This "up-front" coverage for wage-loss, for the first three years after the accident, coupled with immediate payment of medical related expenses, allowed an injured party time to pursue receiving full, fair, and complete compensation for his or her injuries. It also reduced pressure to settle the case early because the injured party was receiving wage-loss compensation and payment of medical expenses.

The other major change contained in the No-Fault Act was that instead of contributory negligence acting as a total bar to an injured party's recovery, an injured party's comparative negligence could be considered to reduce the amount of compensation the injured party received by the percentage of his or her negligence that contributed to the cause of the accident. This means that if an injured party is found to be 25% at-fault (e.g. the injured party was driving too fast), such comparative negligence would not *prevent* the injured party from receiving any compensation for his or her injuries. Rather, such comparative negligence could be taken into consideration by the fact finder, or the insurance adjuster adjusting the claim, to reduce the injured party's compensation award by 25%. For example:

A jury awards the injured party $100,000. The injured party's comparative negligence is set at 25%. The compensation award is then reduced by 25% (in this case, $25,000) resulting in a net award of $75,000 (rather than $0 under the former law).

These three main changes: (1) immediate payment of medical expenses, (2) wage loss coverage (payment of 85% of the injured party's average gross monthly wages, tax-free for three years), and (3) eliminating contributory negligence as a complete bar to recovery, led to Michigan's No-Fault Act being recognized as one of the best insurance programs for citizens in the country.

Under Michigan's No-Fault Act, an injured party who cannot return to work as a result of his or her injuries is typically compensated by his or her own insurance company up to a statutory monthly maximum which, from October 1, 2013 through September 30, 2014 is $5,282 per month. This amount is adjusted for inflation each October. Michigan's No-Fault Act also requires the injured party's own insurance company to reimburse the injured party for his or her reasonable and necessary medical-related expenses for life. Currently, there is no dollar amount limit for medical expenses. Once the injured party's own insurance company's medical-related expenses reach a certain amount, the injured party will continue to receive medical reimbursement from the catastrophic fund established by the No-Fault Act.

It needs to be kept in mind that the greater part of an individual's insurance premium cost covers what is known as first party Personal Injury Protection (PIP). PIP benefits the individual who is paying the insurance premium. Stated another way, the "high cost of motor vehicle insurance" occurs as a result of benefits that are paid primarily to the parties who are injured in motor vehicle accidents. The primary reason for the high cost of motor vehicle insurance is because of the high cost of medical care and the high cost of replacing incomes that are lost when injured parties are unable to continue their employment. PIP benefits are available for the insured, occupants in the insured's motor vehicle, and for individuals who are injured by the operation of a motor vehicle, e.g., a pedestrian, a bicyclist, or a motorcyclist, irrespective of who was at-fault for causing the injury or injuries.

Buying protection for a motor vehicle accident for PIP benefits is similar to buying health insurance or life insurance. It's a social program designed to spread the risk of doing an inherently dangerous act: driving a motor vehicle, even when no other driver contributes to an accident. For example, if someone falls asleep when returning home from a late night event, drives into a tree, and injures herself, her insurance premiums (along with everyone else's) have been structured to pay for her injuries. The rationale being that most people do not drive a motor vehicle intending to injure themselves or others—but when it does happen, that's what insurance is for. In an instant, lives can be turned upside down as a result of motor vehicle accidents. Having a comprehensive insurance program available to Michigan citizens spreads the cost of risks associated with motor vehicle injuries. Underwriters of insurance companies can, and do, charge a fair premium to provide benefits to injured parties guaranteed under Michigan's No-Fault Act.

Accordingly, when individuals complain about the high cost of Michigan's No-Fault motor vehicle insurance, such individuals should keep in mind that the high cost of comprehensive No-Fault insurance in Michigan is primarily due to the medical expenses that need to be paid to properly care for the individuals injured, and to cover economic losses sustained by injured parties for up to the first three years after the accident. The costs of these "benefits" are what drive up premium increases for No-Fault insurance. Injured parties suing other drivers responsible for causing their injuries make up only a small portion of the cost of No-Fault insurance.

Filing Claims against At-Fault Drivers and Their Insurance Companies

Prior to October 1, 1973, if an injured party received a minor injury which caused him to be sore and miss a few days of work, he was able to pursue a claim against the responsible party who caused the accident. Many of these cases resulted in small awards to the injured parties, and acted to clog Michigan's court system.

This all changed with Michigan's No-Fault Act. Now, for an injured party to hold the party who caused the accident responsible for his injuries, he must prove he incurred a wage loss not covered by his PIP coverage, or that he has incurred a serious impairment of a body function (such as walking, talking, smelling, seeing, hearing, or sleeping) or a serious permanent disfigurement. These types of "threshold" injuries allow the injured party to recover non-economic damages (pain and suffering, etc.).

Many court decisions have interpreted just how seriously a body function has to be affected in order to have the injury qualify as a basis for seeking compensation from the party responsible for causing the accident. The spouse of a seriously injured party can also maintain her or his own claim for a "loss of consortium," which is "a derivative claim" based on the spouse's loss of the social pleasures of interacting with her injured spouse. For example, they may no longer be able to go dancing together, or go for walks. Often there is also a major interruption in the parties' conjugal relationship. Additionally, the personal representative of a person who died in a motor vehicle accident also may maintain a claim against the at-fault driver on behalf of the next-of-kin of the deceased.

Collision Costs

Under the No-Fault Act, collision costs are typically the responsibility of the insured driver. This means that when you purchase motor vehicle insurance you either decide to cover your own car and purchase collision coverage, or you chose to run the risk of having your car damaged with little or no recovery. In Michigan, an at-fault driver's liability for damage to your vehicle is currently limited to $1,000 under what is known as the mini-tort provision. Stated another way, in a typical accident, if another driver's motor vehicle collides with your motor vehicle and causes damages, you can only collect up to $1,000 from the at-fault driver, even if the damage to your motor vehicle was $10,000, $20,000, or more.

Accordingly, Michigan places the responsibility of insuring damage to the owner's vehicle on the owner and not on the at-fault driver. There are exceptions to this general rule, such as if the damaged vehicle was legally parked and not being driven when damaged.

Different Types of Insurance Coverage

The No-Fault Act continued the **1963** mandate that any individual registering a motor vehicle in Michigan has to show proof of insurance of at least $20,000 per person and $40,000 per accident to address injuries caused in a motor vehicle accident—this minimum amount of insurance coverage has not changed in over 50 years!! Does that say something about a need to protect yourself from injuries caused by another motor vehicle driver? Fortunately, in Michigan, the owner of any vehicle may purchase insurance coverage for situations where the at-fault driver has no insurance, or has a low limit insurance policy ($20,000) for compensating the injured party. These types of overages are typically referred to as **un**insured coverage or **under**insured coverage. If an individual is seriously injured, suffering a leg amputation or a traumatic brain injury, or killed, $20,000 hardly scratches the surface of properly compensating the injured party, or the injured party's estate. For that reason, having **under**insurance coverage to compensate you if you receive a serious injury from a motor vehicle accident makes sense.

TIP:

To protect yourself from the financial hardship of severe catastrophic injuries, most insurance underwriters offer underinsurance coverage. **(Every Michigan citizen should give serious consideration to purchasing this type of coverage for any vehicle they own.)** If your insurance company does not underwrite underinsurance coverage, I strongly recommend that you consider changing insurance companies to a company that does provide such coverage.

In 2013, political pressure to "save money" on insurance premiums may result in changes to Michigan's No-Fault Law. Most of the concern focuses on the high cost of treating catastrophic injury claims due to brain or spinal cord injuries. From this author's point of view, such changes will, in all likelihood, not be beneficial to citizens in Michigan; keep in mind that, for most people, the high cost of Michigan's motor vehicle insurance is directly related to protecting the drivers of motor vehicles who purchase their own insurance benefits. None of us can escape the fact that the medical cost of traumatic injuries is high, nor can we guarantee that we will never have to face that terrible event.

When a motor vehicle occupant, pedestrian, or motorcyclist is traumatically injured in a motor vehicle accident, they are typically transported to the nearest hospital by ambulance. The ambulance, emergency room, physical therapy, and pain management all cost a significant amount. Michigan's No-Fault PIP benefits, paid into by the owners of motor vehicles through their insurance premiums cover the expenses when a party is injured. From a political standpoint, this is how we have chosen to spread the risk of operating motor vehicles in the State of Michigan. Healthcare providers can count on the fact that when an injured party shows up at their door, an injured party's No-Fault insurance will pay for the medical care that the injured person needs to recover.

If, as is being suggested, a cap is placed on medical expenses for catastrophic injuries, e.g., $300,000, $500,000, or $1,000,000, then consideration should also be given to raising the premiums of liability coverage for the at-fault driver. Accordingly, a change that might make the most sense is <u>to increase</u> the minimum coverage available to those injured. As previously noted, the minimum liability coverage that an insured is required to purchase in order to be allowed to operate a motor vehicle is $20,000 per individual and $40,000 for all individuals injured in one motor vehicle accident (set in 1963). This amount has not gone up in 50 years!

On the other hand, when the No-Fault law was adopted on October 1, 1973, the monthly maximum amount for wage loss was set at $1,000 per month, and indexed to inflation. That maximum amount has increased, as of October 1, 2013to September 30, 2014, to $5,282–over a 500% increase. Applying that same cost of living approach to the $20,000 minimum would put the minimum liability coverage that an insured person should purchase at $100,000 per individual and $200,000 per accident.

Changing Michigan's No-Fault Act to eliminate this protection for injured parties and their medical care providers will be a step back in Michigan's motor vehicle insurance laws—a bad change to one of the best insurance programs in the nation for providing care to injured parties of motor vehicle accidents. We must remember that motor vehicle insurance is a social program designed to spread the risk of caring for injured parties in motor vehicle accidents. Motor vehicle insurance companies should not be solely in the business of "making money" for their shareholders. That is why we have an insurance commissioner to make sure that all policies are fairly written to protect individuals, and to ensure that the benefits provided under such policies are actually provided to injured parties and their medical care providers by the insurance carriers.

Chapter 1

Where to Start

I have been injured, or a person I love has
been injured or a loved one has been killed.
What should I do now?

*For every motor vehicle accident, when you or a person you love has
been injured, or when a loved one has died, there are actions that
need to be undertaken immediately in order to obtain the best results
for those affected by injury or death.*

Understanding the Terms

Michigan's No-Fault law is set forth at MCL 500.3101-
500.3179. MCL references in this book refer to sections of
the No-Fault law contained in Michigan Complied Laws.
Sections of Michigan's No-Fault law are set forth in statutes
adopted by Michigan's Legislature. Each section is then
"interpreted" by Michigan courts, and in individual cases
such sections are applied to the unique facts of the no-fault
claim presented.

In every motor vehicle accident, the **first party** is your insurance company or the insurance company, under priority rules, responsible for paying your Personal Injury Protection (PIP) benefits. To register a motor vehicle, every Michigan motor vehicle owner is required, by law, to purchase first party PIP benefits. PIP benefits provide money for such things as:

- **Work loss** for the first three years after the accident;
- Reimbursement for **replacement services** (hiring people to do things for you that you were previously able to do but can no longer can perform due to accident-related injuries). These replacement services include lawn care, child care, snow shoveling, grocery shopping, and household chores. Reimbursement for the cost of replacement services is available for up to three years after the accident; and
    - Reimbursement for **medical-related expenses <u>for life,</u>** and, if necessary, for home attendant care (up to 24 hours a day), for life.

PIP benefits are available <u>regardless</u> of whether the injured party was at-fault in causing the accident, and that's part of the reason why Michigan's Motor Vehicle Insurance Law is referred to as "No-Fault Insurance."

In every motor vehicle accident where an individual has been injured or killed, the injured party or the decedent's estate is referred to as the **second party**. If the **second**

party was injured or killed as the result of the negligence of another, then another person, the "at-fault party" and his or her insurance company is collectively referred to as the **third party.** Obviously, if the injured or deceased party was involved in a single vehicle accident, (e.g., the driver fell asleep, ran off the road, and hit a tree), then there is no **third party**. So, briefly:

1. First party: your insurance company providing PIP benefits

2. Second party: the injured person

3. Third party: the person at-fault, and his or her insurance company

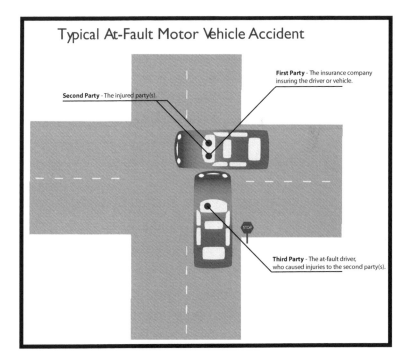

Typical At-Fault Motor Vehicle Accident

First Party - The insurance company insuring the driver or vehicle.

Second Party - The injured party(s).

Third Party - The at-fault driver, who caused injuries to the second party(s).

It's important to keep in mind an understanding of these terms: first party, second party, and third party, as you review the material in this book. Many of the important benefits you are entitled to receive in every motor vehicle accident come from your own insurance company. Obtaining those benefits, however, even from your own insurance company, can often be as difficult as obtaining compensation from an at-fault third party driver and his insurance company.

Whether or not you will receive benefits and compensation is critically dependent on providing all the necessary documentation. This is true for either type of claim—a **first party** claim filed with your own insurance company or a **third party** claim against the responsible third party driver and his or her insurance company. Keep good records by following my recommendations below. There are also times when the **first party** insurance company (usually your own insurance carrier unless you were driving or riding on a motorcycle) and the **third party** insurance company are the same. In such cases, it is usually best to demand that separate insurance adjusters be assigned to your **first party** claim and your **third party** claim, and not to allow sharing of the respective files.

Documenting your injuries, and your economic losses (wages, replacement services, etc.), your pain, and your suffering and mental anguish will help you carry the day with your claim. Failing to document such issues will seriously diminish the value of your claim.

First Critical Steps

1. Immediately, document how the accident occurred. Someone, either the injured party or a person acting on behalf of the injured or deceased party, must document how the motor vehicle accident occurred and who was, and who was not, at-fault in causing your injuries. Such documentation will determine whether the at-fault driver's insurance company will pay a claim for compensation for such things as:

- wage loss in excess of PIP benefits;
- pain and suffering, and other non-economic damages suffered by an injured party; and
- for the loss of the love, society, and companionship of a person wrongfully killed by someone's negligence.

TIP:

Do **not** rely solely on the police and the police report to fully document how the accident occurred. If there is any question as to who was at-fault in causing the accident, or what occurred during the accident, consideration should be given to hiring an independent and experienced accident reconstruction expert and a private investigator to question witnesses.

2. While doing everything possible to recover from your injuries, you should also document all of your efforts to do so, and the expenses you incur in the process.

3. I cannot stress strongly enough how critical it may be to your claim or to the claim of a loved one to take immediate steps to contact an experienced motor vehicle accident attorney to discuss whether to immediately hire an accident reconstruction expert. Sadly, if an expert is prevented from examining evidence because the evidence has been destroyed or lost, a party's **third party** claim may also suffer a similar fate, to wit: the claim may be disallowed or lost since such claim will not be provable.

The accident reconstruction expert can only offer opinion testimony on evidence that has been preserved. The accident reconstruction expert reconstructs how the accident occurred based on reviewing photos, taking measurements, and personally examining physical evidence. If photos were not taken, or were not taken from the correct angle, and with the necessary magnification, evidence may be forever lost. If the damage to the vehicles was not examined before repairs were made, evidence may be lost. If the tires, brakes, trailers, or trailer hitches were not physically examined to assess their proper functioning at the time of the crash, evidence may be lost.

After a phone call from an experienced motor vehicle accident attorney, an accident reconstruction expert can often be dispatched to the scene of an accident to gather evidence. Sometimes this is possible the day of or the day after an accident or within a few days thereof. Having the accident reconstruction expert immediately dispatched often allows the expert to review evidence which has remained at the actual scene of the accident. What the expert views can be used to say whether the accident happened in a particular way. Allowing the expert to take photos of the road surface, the markings that may have been left on the traveled portion or the shoulder of the road (e.g., "yaw marks"), may well tell a different story as to how the accident happened than what may have been described according to witness accounts.

Retaining an experienced motor vehicle accident expert allows an attorney to take the necessary steps to ensure that possible important evidence is preserved. The attorney can contact authorities to make sure that evidence is not released without first having an expert representing the injured or deceased person examine the same. If necessary, the motor vehicle accident attorney can go to court and obtain orders restraining persons and agencies from destroying or removing evidence and allowing for vehicles involved in the accident to be examined by an independent expert before such vehicles are repaired.

Sometimes the vehicle involved in causing the accident may have had a mechanical condition that contributed to the cause of the accident. In a rare case, it is possible that even a one-car accident might have been caused by the negligence of a third party, e.g., an auto repair shop that negligently failed to properly bolt newly installed tires. Normally, however, it is the negligence of a **third party driver**, <u>and</u> the vehicle that was being driven by the **third party driver** that needs to be documented. If the motor vehicle driven by the **third party** was being driven at a time when it was unsafe, then documenting such unsafe condition could be critical.

It is also possible that the police may not have interviewed all of the witnesses who were at the scene of the motor vehicle accident. Sometimes, what is said or done immediately after the accident maybe very relevant in apportioning negligence between the drivers. Asking witnesses relevant questions by an experienced private investigator can be extremely crucial in explaining what did or did not happen in the accident and whether a party experienced conscience pain and suffering after being injured but prior to dying from his or her injuries.

Three Case Studies:
Why You Should Immediately Contact an Experienced Motor Vehicle Attorney to Protect Physical Evidence

Case 1

In a wrongful death case which I was involved in, the family of the deceased person came to see me within days after the truck accident occurred. From all initial reports, the deceased, a responsible 16-year-old girl, was deemed <u>solely</u> at-fault for the accident that led to her death. She pulled out in front of a semi-truck that broadsided her vehicle. Police reports tended to exculpate the truck driver from <u>any</u> wrongdoing, and no criminal charges were filed as a result of her death. Nevertheless, the parents of the deceased had serious questions as to how their daughter, whom they believed to be a very responsible driver, had been solely at-fault by pulling out in front of the oncoming truck.

After I became involved, I contacted the owner of the semi-truck and requested that he voluntarily agree to keep the damaged truck at the storage facility where it had been towed so that I could have it inspected. He refused my request. I immediately obtained a restraining order requiring that the truck be secured at the collision storage facility until I could have it examined for motor vehicle defects, most notably, the truck's braking system. I contacted an air brake expert in Salt Lake City, Utah, and flew him to Michigan to examine the truck. I also retained the services of an accident reconstruction expert to help me and the family understand how this tragic accident had occurred.

After having the truck examined, it was determined that approximately two-thirds of the vehicle's twenty-four air brakes were not functioning properly at the time of the accident. This meant that when the brakes were applied only one-third of the air brake drums actually engaged to slow the vehicle. This same expert was able to testify that had even half of the non-functioning air brakes been properly working, the accident in question would likely have been avoided. Had all of the air brakes been properly functioning, the opinion of the expert was, without question, that the collision would not have occurred, and my client's precious daughter might still be alive today. Had the truck been repaired, all of the evidence regarding the negligent maintenance of the brakes would have been lost.

Additionally, the accident reconstruction expert was puzzled by the construction of the intersection. After examining extensive documents from the State of Michigan, it was also determined by the expert that the intersection was unsafe. Documents obtained from the State's archives demonstrated that when the intersection was constructed major safety concerns were not addressed, and even though the planning documents called for a large hill to the west to be leveled the leveling never occurred.

Though no criminal charges were filed by the authorities, during litigation, a very sizeable settlement was secured on behalf of the estate of the deceased girl. To the credit of the deceased's family, a smaller settlement was obtained from the State of Michigan *conditioned* on a written agreement that the intersection be redesigned according to the safety standards that should have been followed in the first place.

The intersection was redesigned, including adding a new lane and leveling the hill to the west. It was clear from the accident reconstruction expert's point of view, that my client's child had not been able to see the truck to the west due to the hill and a steep incline. The truck being in the far right lane was out of my client's daughter's view as she started to pull out into the intersection. Prior to the truck coming into the intersection, the truck was changing lanes and speeding up, even though a yellow caution light was blinking to warn drivers of the dangerousness of this intersection.

Oftentimes, the **third party's** insurance company will claim that either you or your loved one was negligent in causing your injuries or your loved one's death. In Michigan, as stated in the introduction, this is called comparative negligence. If you or the deceased driver can be shown to be more than 50% at-fault for causing the accident, then even though a **third party** may also have been at-fault in causing the accident, you may be denied a **third party** recovery. Had the family of this 16-year-old driver not immediately contacted me, it is doubtful that the truck involved would ever have been properly inspected to document the seriousness of the brake failure. In addition, the State of Michigan would not have redesigned the intersection.

Due the family's efforts and their concern for the safety of others, a once very dangerous intersection (where a number of people had been previously killed as a result of motor vehicle accidents), has now been free of any traffic fatalities since the intersection was redesigned. As of the writing of this book, that was over 15 years ago!

Case 2

My client, an emergency medical technician (EMT), was riding in an ambulance transporting an injured man to a hospital in Saginaw. During the ride, the injured man voiced his concern about pain due to the placement of his intravenous therapy (IV). My client unbuckled her seat belt to adjust the IV tubes, and at that moment an oncoming vehicle crossed the center line and struck the ambulance, causing it to roll over. Before the ambulance came to rest, the back doors of the ambulance flew open and ejected both the patient on the gurney and my client.

Tragically, the patient died and my client's right leg was crushed by the ambulance during the rollover. My client's injuries were so severe her right leg had to be amputated above her knee. This accident occurred in February, a week before my client was to be married. I recall being called by family members and being asked to travel to the hospital in Saginaw to answer questions regarding insurance documents which a representative from her insurance company wanted her to sign.

I drove to Saginaw on a very snowy night to visit with my client and her family. After answering questions, I inquired about what specifically she recalled about the accident. She answered to the best of her ability but, as she was inside the back of the ambulance when it was struck, her recollection was obviously limited.

After meeting with the family, the big question in my mind was why both my client and her patient had been ejected from the ambulance. Accordingly, **the very next day** I contacted the hospital which employed my client and requested two things:

1. That the damaged ambulance be secured and preserved for future inspection.
2. That I be allowed to view the ambulance myself as soon as possible.

I very carefully explained that I believed it was in the hospital's best interest to agree to my request to protect both themselves and to also potentially help one of their employees. Workers' compensation would cover my client's injuries insofar as the hospital was concerned, but my client just might have a possible claim against the manufacturer of the ambulance if something was wrong with how the vehicle had been constructed. Again, I just couldn't figure out why both ambulance doors would have just "flown open" during the accident.

The hospital agreed to both of my requests.

I went to the storage facility where the ambulance had been taken. I examined the damaged ambulance and came away with a "gut feeling" that something was indeed wrong with the doors of the ambulance. Even though during the accident, the ambulance had rolled over on its side, there was actually very little damage to most of the ambulance, especially to the doors at the back of the ambulance.

After the accident, the family of the patient who had been killed retained a personal injury attorney to represent the patient's estate. I knew this attorney and I had a great deal of respect for him and his judgment. After my ambulance visit, I contacted the attorney representing the estate of the deceased patient. When we met, I shared with him my concerns about the "crashworthiness" of the ambulance, and how this might have contributed to both the death of his client and to the severe injuries received by my client.

Even though his clients and my client had different legal issues (he had a possible negligence claim against the hospital, while, due to worker's compensation, my client did not), both clients could possibly have a product defect liability claim against the manufacturer of the ambulance.

As a result of our clients' mutual interest, a partnership of sorts was formed. We both shared the expense of retaining the services of a safety expert from Chrysler Corporation. The safety expert reviewed the photos I had taken and agreed there might be an issue to investigate.

Thereafter, the safety expert traveled to Isabella County and inspected the ambulance. He took his own set of detailed photos, took measurements, made calibrations, documented the damages, and more importantly, the lack of damages, to the rear door area and to the locking mechanism of the ambulance's rear doors.

The safety expert was able to perform tests proving that the "newly installed" locking system which had been recently engineered by the manufacturer, opened too easily under pressure. After his examination, his opinion corroborated my suspicions. It was his determination that the doors' locking systems failed to adhere to federal motor vehicle safety standards which required the locking mechanism of the rear doors to be able to withstand a certain amount of force (and pressure) before opening.

As a result of preserving the evidence, four things occurred:

1. An expert was able to document a major contributing factor which caused my client's injuries and a patient's death.
2. A third party product defect liability claim against the manufacturer was able to be documented.
3. A substantial amount of money was paid by the ambulance manufacturer to my client and to the family of the deceased patient to compensate each party for their loss.
4. A voluntary nationwide recall occurred resulting in hundreds of ambulances being recalled to have their locking systems reconfigured. This likely resulted in saving many lives and prevented similar types of injuries.

As a side note, the at-fault driver who had struck the ambulance was a young college student who only possessed a $20,000/$40,000 liability policy. Had there been no product liability claim preserved and developed against the manufacturer of the ambulance, compensation for my client's catastrophic injuries would have been limited to a certain number of weeks of "loss compensation" pursuant to the Workers' Compensation Act. My client would have received virtually nothing for her pain, suffering, and other non-economic losses.

Case 3

My client was involved in a motor vehicle accident where a young boy was killed. In that accident, the truck my client was driving came into contact with the bicycle the boy was riding. Initially, the police believed the truck ran into the boy's bicycle as the boy was riding to school at approximately 7:30 a.m. to 8:00 a.m.

Initially, my client was charged with negligent homicide. He was also later sued by the child's estate for the child's wrongful death.

After reading the police report and talking with my client, (this was prior to retaining the experts I cite below) I had one picture in my mind as to how the accident had occurred. The picture in my mind wasn't one that I felt would help my client under the circumstances.

Again, things aren't always as they appear. I immediately sought help from the services of an experienced independent accident reconstruction expert. I also retained the services of a conspicuity expert. A conspicuity expert is an expert in the sub-specialty field of psychology who can offer opinion testimony as to why people see or do not see something before them. A conspicuity expert would be able to possibly help me to explain why my client was not able to see the boy on the bicycle who was riding on or near the edge of the highway prior to the accident.

After the evidence was examined by the experts, and after their opinions were shared with me, a much different picture emerged of what had happened (and yes, more importantly, what had <u>not</u> happened).

Picture Before Experts Were Retained

Picture After Experts Were Retained

The above facts painted quite a different picture of the accident scene. Added to this picture was a set of oncoming headlights of the vehicle cresting the hill from northbound lane, which was veering towards the center line after cresting (per the testimony of the 16-year-old driver who stated that she "always pulled over to the right" as she approached a hill and once she crested the hill she drove back left towards the center of the road).

This 16-year-old's testimony allowed the conspicuity expert to testify at court that the oncoming truck driver's eyes would have been "focused," out of fear, to a 5% degree of acuity on the headlights of the car coming toward his lane. The cumulative effect of the truck driver focusing on the approaching danger of the vehicle moving toward the center of the roadway (and towards his lane of travel), together with the lack of any visibility or contrast on the part of the bicyclist, provided the foundation for the conspicuity expert testifying at trial that there was "no way possible" that the truck driver ever saw, or more importantly, <u>could</u> <u>have</u> even seen the bicyclist prior to impact.

The accident reconstruction expert also testified that, based on how the accident was documented, there was no way to tell whether it was the bicyclist who had actually turned into the path of the truck driver.

It was also the accident reconstruction expert who discovered that workers for the county road commission had mismarked the center line on the roadway. This caused the southbound traveled portion (between the white lines marking each outer edge of the north and southbound lanes), to be only nine feet wide, when it should have been 10 feet wide. Considering the fact that the truck was eight feet, six inches wide, the extra 12 inches not available for driving was likely a critical factor contributing to the cause of this tragic accident.

The conspicuity expert and I traveled to the sheriff's department and photographed the clothing that had been worn by the deceased boy at the time of the accident. The conspicuity expert used equipment to measure the clothing's light absorption factor versus its light reflecting factor. The dark clothes also exacerbated the lack of contrast that naturally occurs in early morning light. Making visibility matters worse, there was also a light mist in the air.

The accident reconstruction expert also went to the sheriff's department and examined the damaged bicycle that the young boy was riding at the time of the accident. Sadly, it was determined that when someone assembled the bike, or maintained the bike, they inadvertently turned the rear reflector upside down: it was positioned below the seat and below the rear fender so it would not have been visible to reflect light that came from behind the bicycle.

Had these two experts not been retained to develop the evidence that was there to be developed, (but had not been developed during the police investigation), there is no doubt in my mind that an innocent man would have been convicted of a crime that he did not commit.

The jury took less than one hour to return a "not guilty" verdict against my client. Had my client been convicted, he would have lost his job as a state building inspector who traveled to construction sites throughout Michigan to evaluate compliance with construction contracts—which would have been a devastating financial loss. Had he been convicted, he would have been wrongfully labeled a criminal, and likely spent six months to a year in jail as punishment for his crime of negligent homicide.

Coincidentally, the evidence gathered to protect my client from being wrongfully convicted of a crime also provided potential evidence to assist the estate of the deceased boy in pursuing a third party negligence claim against the country road commission for mismarking the roadway where the accident occurred.

The bottom line: Justice can be better served by taking quick action to contact an experienced motor vehicle accident attorney to preserve and develop evidence. Employing accident reconstruction experts, biomechanical experts, and motor vehicle experts, such as the air brake expert and conspicuity expert, can determine whether you have a viable claim against a third party who is responsible for causing the accident.

Two Categories of Claims: Injury Claims and Wrongful Death Claims

For obvious reasons, it is helpful to break down actions to be taken by you, or on behalf of a person you love, into two broad categories.

1. Actions to take when you or a person you love has been seriously <u>injured</u> result of a motor vehicle accident..

2. Actions to take when a loved one has <u>died</u> as a result of a motor vehicle accident.

What To Do in The Case of Injuries

First, let's take a look what you should do to build your case in the first scenario: you or a person you love has been seriously injured in a motor vehicle accident.

1. *Do everything possible to get better.*
   After being injured, the most important thing for you to do is to recover from your injury. Follow the suggestions of qualified medical personnel. It may sound obvious, but do what your doctor or physical therapist tells you to do.

   Keep all follow-up appointments. Don't try to heal on your own. I can't tell you how many times an insurance adjuster or a defense attorney will place blame on the injured party (you), for not following through with follow-up physical therapy appointments, follow-up doctor's appointments, etc.

Injured parties who try to "tough it out" end up being penalized for their efforts to recover. If you visit with a doctor and the doctor or a member of his or her staff ask you to rate your pain from 1 to 10, and you try to minimize your pain to show them how tough you are, e.g., rating it as a 1 or a 2 when you really could just as easily rate it as a 6 or a 7, will come back to haunt you. Your own insurance adjuster, or the insurance company's representative of the third party, will point out how well you were doing on a particular doctor visit. Just be honest. Do not under-report or over-report the pain and discomfort you are experiencing as a result of your injuries.

2. *The law requires you to "mitigate" your damages.*

In other words, the law requires you to do that which is necessary to improve your physical condition and recover from your injuries. In such regard, this may mean taking one or all of the following actions:

- *Be sure to tell your doctor what hurts.* Ultimately, the dollar value placed on your loss, will greatly depend on the evaluation of your medical records. We call such evidence "documented medical evidence." Your doctor, intake nurse, or physician's assistant is required to detail, using your own words, your reported statements on "how you feel" and how your injuries have affected you. Reporting in detail, to your medical providers, what you can't do because of your injuries will help document whether you have suffered a serious impairment of a body function. For example: "I can't sleep anymore in a bed. I have to sleep in a reclining chair. I can't walk without pain. I can't go to the bathroom without assistance. I can't turn my head to the right." The more detailed your reporting is to your medical care providers, the stronger your claim will be!

TIP:

Think of the detailed reporting as a way to provide your doctors with the best information to help them design a treatment plan that will speed your recovery.

- ***Do not miss appointments with your doctor.***
  Stay in touch with your doctor and be
  certain to maintain your appointments. If
  you have to cancel, notify the doctor with
  as much advance notice as possible and give
  the reasons for the cancellation. The words
  "no show" in a doctor's records can be used
  against you when trying to reach a fair
  settlement or at trial.

- ***Attend all physical therapy (PT) sessions as
  prescribed.*** Your physician or hospital staff
  may prescribe physical therapy to help you
  recover from your injury. PT is often helpful
  for many types of injuries, including strains,
  sprains and other so-called *soft tissue* injuries. If
  physical therapy is prescribed, be sure to keep
  your appointments and participate actively in
  the process. Again, if you have to cancel an
  appointment, be sure to call in advance and
  explain the reason for the cancellation. That
  being said, it's best to avoid cancellations as
  much as possible.

- ***Within reason, do what your doctor tells you
  to do.*** If your physician prescribes certain
  medications, therapy exercises, or limitations
  of activities, be sure to follow your doctor's
  orders. Failure to adhere to your doctor's
  advice can be used against you when it comes
  time to settle your case and it can be used

against you in court if your claim actually proceeds to litigation.

- ***Follow your doctor's advice with respect to work and leisure activities.*** If your physician advises you to rest, stay at home from work, or avoid certain types of activities, it's important that you follow such advice. If you resist your doctor's advice, and engage in activities that you have been told to avoid, it will not only prevent your speedy recovery, but it could also affect the legal aspects of your case. Even though staying out of work may have an impact financially, it is important that you follow such advice so that your recovery will be enhanced. If you have problems obtaining compensation from your own insurance company, an attorney can assist you to recover medical expenses not reimbursed or wages lost.

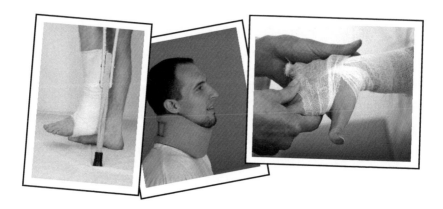

3. *Take photos and videos of your injuries and how your injuries have reduced or diminished your quality of life.*

In addition to documenting how your motor vehicle accident occurred, and the potential negligence claim against any third party, it also extremely important to pictorially document the nature and extent of your injuries. It is often said that a picture is worth a thousand words. Hospital photographs of you or your loved one who has been injured in the accident will help document the nature and extent of you or your loved one's injuries.

If at all possible, I typically recommend taking a live video in the hospital room where you or your loved one describes the pain that he or she is currently experiencing. An audio description captured on video will help convey to any third party claims adjuster (or potentially to a jury down the road if your case has to be litigated) how your injuries have affected you, in terms of pain and suffering, and mental anguish. Thereafter, in your home, at the physical therapy office, and in other locations, take additional videos documenting a day in your life *after* the accident. Such recordings will be very helpful to document the full nature and extent of your injuries.

The more professional these video and audio documentations are, the better the result you will have in obtaining a settlement you deserve to compensate you for all that you have had to go through as a result of someone else's negligence.

4. *Contacted by an insurance adjuster? Politely defer comment until you have spoken with an attorney.*

You may be contacted by an adjuster from your own insurance company as well as someone acting on behalf of the insurance company of the third party who was at-fault in causing your accident. My best advice is to politely indicate to anyone contacting you in the hospital or shortly after you have returned home that you would like to seek the advice of an attorney experienced in handling motor vehicle accident cases before making any comments.

Politely advise your own insurance adjuster that you appreciate them contacting you and that you will get back to them as soon as you have had an opportunity to consult with someone familiar with how to best protect you in light of your accident. Your own insurance company's adjuster may certainly be trying to be helpful, but he or she may not realize that your statements might later be misconstrued by a third party insurance adjuster. The third party adjuster may review your insurance company notes in his or her deliberations on their company's obligation to compensate you for non-economic benefits such as r pain, suffering, and mental anguish.

While you have an obligation to notify your insurance company soon after a motor vehicle accident of your accident and your injuries, you have no <u>immediate</u> obligation to give a recorded statement to anyone. I strongly recommend that you consult with an attorney well-versed in handling motor vehicle accidents before making any statements (recorded or otherwise), to anyone, other than those already likely made to the police officer at the scene of the motor vehicle accident.

5. *Paying your medical bills.*

Keep in mind that Michigan's No-Fault law is one of the best in the nation for making sure that the medical bills you incur as a result of a motor vehicle accident will be paid. Subject to deductibles, all of your out of pocket expense should be covered by your motor vehicle insurance company, or a combination of your motor vehicle insurance company and your health insurance provider.

There are two types of motor vehicle coverage available: coordinated coverage and uncoordinated coverage.

Coordinated coverage: If you have healthcare insurance, your motor vehicle insurance carrier will "coordinate" coverage with your health insurance provider, and both parties will help cover your medical costs (after deductibles). Your health care insurance will cover most of your medical bills, but your motor vehicle insurance will cover any medical expenses not covered by your health insurance—including things like modifications to your home such as ramps for wheelchair access. Generally, coordinated motor vehicle coverage has a lower premium as medical costs are defrayed by two insurance companies.

Uncoordinated coverage: If you have an "uncoordinated" policy because you do not have health insurance, then subject to deductibles your medical expenses will be covered 100% by your own motor vehicle policy if you were involved in a motor vehicle collision. Uncoordinated policies generally have a higher premium as the motor vehicle insurance company is responsible for all medical expenses.

If you were a passenger injured in a motor vehicle accident, medical payments may also be available from the drivers or the owners of the vehicle(s) involved who have motor vehicle insurance. If you do not have any insurance coverage, it is possible that your personal funds could be required to pay for medical bills as well. Workers compensation insurance may be available to you if you were working on the job and the injury occurred as a result of your employment.

Additionally, the liability insurance coverage of the insurance company for the third party, if another party was at-fault for causing your injuries, can also be made available to you, if you have no other type of insurance coverage available. Some insurance coverage benefits will be paid at the time of settlement, rather than during the period that you incur the medical bills. Depending on the nature of your case, your medical bills may be covered by any of the previously mentioned methods. If you have no insurance coverage, you should save copies of all of your bills, and, if a third party is responsible, hopefully the medical bills will be paid at a later date when, and if, your third party claim settles with a favorable result for you.

In most cases, when there is no <u>immediate</u> method to pay medical bills as they are being incurred, many doctors, hospitals, and other medical care facilities will wait to be paid for their services until your case is finally resolved by way of a settlement or verdict in court if you have a third party claim. It is important to let medical providers know early in the process if you have no insurance or financial means to pay the medical bills as they are being incurred and that you have a third party claim against another individual (and their insurance company). You should also notify medical providers that you have retained legal counsel, if such is the case, to assist you with pursuing your third party claim. Most insurance companies for the third party will not automatically pay medical bills as they occur, even when there is clear liability on the part of the third party. Most liability insurance companies will wait for a demand letter from your attorney, and then try to conclude the case all at once with one payment. In most motor vehicle accidents (unless you were riding a motorcycle), your own auto insurance carrier will be responsible for paying all reasonable and necessary medically-related expenses (prescriptions, physical therapy care, doctor and hospital bills, etc.).

One of the most important things for you to do is to keep an accurate record of your medical bills. It is important that you do the following:

- Ask for a medical bill each time you see a doctor or facility. Maintain a record of your visits and make sure that you obtain a medical bill for each visit to your doctor, hospital, physical therapist, or medical facility.

- Save all prescription bills. Be sure to save copies of your prescription and drug store charges for medicine that you purchase as a result of your injury.

- Keep a separate record with appointment dates, amounts of medical bills, services, purchases for medication, and how the bills were paid (by insurance, your own personal funds, etc.) that summarizes all events. This requirement is very important because it will be your actual record of medical bills incurred as a result of your injuries.

- If you retain a lawyer to help you recover a settlement for your case, be sure that your lawyer receives a copy of each medical bill, prescription bill, or other bill related to your injury.

It is important for any lawyer you retain to receive copies of all of medical bills, as well as a copy of your medical bills summary when your case is ready for settlement. Even though your lawyer may receive copies of bills from your medical facilities, a double check will assure that your claim settles for the maximum value. If your lawyer does not have a copy of all your medical bills, your case may settle for less than its actual value. "Specials" include your out-of-pocket expenses such as medical expenses. Many insurance companies utilize a multiple of the total dollars of your "specials" as a measure of the value of your case (e.g. two or three times your specials).

Although this approach is used less often than in the past, it remains a factor for many insurance adjusters. Save your bills and submit them to your attorney at reasonable intervals (rather than <u>each</u> time you receive them), unless a particular bill is for a significant sum, say, several thousand dollars for a lengthy hospital stay.

6. *Other Suggestions:*

If you are reading this to educate yourself about to how to respond should you have the misfortune of being in a motor vehicle accident then let me add these recommendations: at the scene of the auto accident, obtain a list of witnesses who could testify about your injuries or about how the accident occurred; have someone take photographs of you at the accident scene or as soon as possible after the accident; and <u>if you have an attorney in whom you have confidence who regularly handles motor vehicle accident cases, notify his or her law firm immediately after the accident while you are recovering.</u> If you are hospitalized, the attorney may begin gathering evidence immediately before it is lost and while you are being treated for your injuries. Typically, the attorney or someone from the attorney's office will meet with you immediately and request that you sign certain forms so that they can obtain information as soon as possible regarding your medical records and employment records.

I would also suggest that, if you are a parent, you share all this knowledge with the new drivers in your family. The first time your son or daughter is in a motor vehicle accident—even if it is only a minor one—can be a very frightening experience for him or her and you. Having some knowledge *beforehand* about how to respond in the event of an accident might reduce the anxiety level if something does happen.

What to Do in the Case of Wrongful Death

Now, let's take a look what you should do to build your case in the second scenario: when a loved one has died as the result of a motor vehicle accident.

1. **A loved one's estate may have a cause of action for monetary compensation for the decedent's pain, suffering, and mental anguish experienced <u>after</u> being injured but <u>before</u>**

death. In the case of a seriously injured person who dies days later, this component of damages may be significant, especially if the injuries inflicted to your loved one caused the decedent to experience a painful death (e.g. your loved one was burned extensively during the motor vehicle crash). If at all possible, documenting the nature and extent of your loved one's injuries, after the accident, but <u>before</u> death should be attempted. Again, if at all possible, take photos and videos as previously discussed in the case of an injured loved one. Photos and videos can be very helpful later when documenting what pain and suffering was likely experienced by your loved one prior to his or her death.

Obviously, this documentation must take a back seat to any medical efforts being undertaken to save the life of your loved one. But, if someone can take photos and videos without interfering with efforts of the medical personnel to save the life of your loved one, such documentation will be most helpful (and equally useful to your loved one if they survive their life-threatening injuries).

2. **Upon the death of your loved one, a probate estate must be opened.** Michigan law provides that a personal representative of your loved one's estate needs to be appointed by a probate court judge in the county where your loved one lived (or if he or

she resided outside of the State of Michigan, a probate estate can be opened in the state where he or she lived). A personal representative represents the estate of your loved one to maintain and settle any claims your loved one and his next of kin may have for the decedent's wrongful death. Immediately contacting an attorney who is experienced with handling motor vehicle accidents can be critical to whether your loved one's estate recovers for a wrongful death.

3. **If your loved one had a properly drafted will, your loved one named someone to be his or her personal representative and likely also named an alternative personal representative.** Assuming that such named person is available and willing, then he or she will most likely be the individual appointed by the court to be the personal representative of your loved one's estate.

If your loved one died without a will (intestate), then Michigan law prioritizes who should be the personal representative. If a minor child has died, then that child's parents (either the mother or the father) collectively have first priority, and the deceased's adult siblings would have a secondary prioritization. If an adult has died, and leaves no surviving spouse or adult children, then the adult's parents collectively have the highest priority with adult siblings equally sharing a secondary prioritization. If an adult dies, and has a spouse, then the adult spouse has the highest priority, with any adult children of the deceased adult having equal secondary prioritization.

Ultimately, the individual with the highest priority is likely to end up being appointed by the court to be the personal representative of your loved one's estate. Divorced parents share equally with the priority of their deceased child, regardless of who had primary custody of any minor child. Once a personal representative for the estate of your loved one has been identified, that individual should be the person to move forward to protect the interests of the loved one's estate and family left behind.

The personal representative will be the individual who primarily works with attorneys, claims adjusters, and the court to resolve all possible claims that can be made on behalf of the deceased's estate. The personal representative will also represent those persons entitled to maintain a claim for their own individual loss of society and companionship as a result of the wrongful death of the deceased.

4. **The personal representative of the loved one's estate needs to act, as quickly as possible, to secure the advice of an experienced personal injury attorney who regularly handles motor vehicle accidents.** Depending on the unique facts of your loved one's death and available compensation to adjust the various claims, an experienced personal injury attorney is usually the best individual to advise you about what steps the personal representative should take to protect the claims of all individuals affected by your loved one's death.

Normally, retaining an experienced personal injury attorney to represent the estate's interests is the best and most prudent decision that can be made by the personal representative. Obtaining the assistance of an attorney to explore all possible options for insurance coverage to adjust the claim can be critical. The attorney will know what questions to ask and how to find the answers. For example:

- Is there underinsurance coverage available from the first party's insurance carrier when there is minimal insurance coverage available from the third party's insurance carrier (e.g. $20,000)?

- Can insurance companies' coverage be "stacked" between the third party driver and the motor vehicle owner whose vehicle was being operated at the time of the accident?
- Are there any third party defendants, other than a driver who could be responsible, in part, for the death of your loved one (e.g., a dram shop claim against an establishment that furnished alcohol to the driver of the other vehicle at a time when the driver was visibly impaired)?

5. **When an individual has died, Michigan has a statute referred to as the *Wrongful Death Statute*.** The Wrongful Death Statute defines which individuals can make a claim for their personal individual loss of society and companionship as a result of the wrongful death of another human being. A spouse, parents, grandparents, children, and siblings can each maintain a claim for their personal loss. Deciding who should receive what amount of monetary compensation to compensate such individuals for their personal loss can be a very difficult and emotional process. Again, having the advice of an experienced personal injury attorney who regularly handles motor vehicle accidents can be extremely helpful in addressing this issue.

When your loved one was a wage earner and helping to support his or her spouse and/or a minor child or children, the loss of the decedent's economic support is also something that the estate can pursue in a civil action to compensate those individuals affected by such loss. When your loved one died as a result of someone else's negligence, monetary compensation, though woefully inadequate, is the only thing available to compensate you and others directly affected by the wrongful death of your loved one. Obtaining such financial compensation, however, can be extremely important to help raise young children and support a spouse who has lost a wage earner who would have helped support them in life.

6. **The personal representative should act quickly** to select an experienced personal injury attorney who regularly represents motor vehicle accident victims <u>in the area where the deceased lived,</u> or, in some cases, where the motor vehicle accident occurred.

This person will need to quickly gather information to document how the accident occurred, to preserve evidence that might otherwise be lost, and if necessary, to hire experts to prove what did, or often just as importantly, what did not occur when the accident happened. There may be legal and factual issues of comparative negligence or proximate causation that need to be documented and nailed down quickly. Sadly, as discussed previously, if evidence is not gathered quickly it may be forever lost. Evidence at the accident scene itself may be lost if not photographed, gathered, etc.

7. **The personal representative of the deceased's estate needs to work with the personal injury attorney to document the loss of those individuals entitled to make a claim.** Those individuals, as stated, could include the personal representative making a claim on behalf of the estate if the loved one incurred pain and suffering prior to his or her death after being injured in the motor vehicle accident. Additionally, those individuals under the Wrongful Death Statute who are entitled to make a claim—the next-of-kin—need to have their loss of society and companionship documented. The personal representative will need to help the personal injury attorney understand the emotional ties that existed between the deceased and those individuals entitled to make claims under Michigan's Wrongful Death Statute. Initially, benefits for funeral and burial expenses are payable in the amount set forth in the insured's insurance policy. The amount payable cannot be less than $1,750 or more than $5,000.

Additionally, should the deceased leave behind a surviving spouse and/or minor children who were dependent on income earned by the deceased, then their economic loss will also have to be calculated and documented. Their economic loss for the first three years after the decedent's death is typically referred to as "survivor loss benefits."

Survivor loss benefits include financial support that the decedent's dependents would have received from the deceased, together with up to $20 per day for replacement services that the deceased would have performed. The amount recoverable for replacement services is then combined with the amount recoverable for the loss of financial support provided by the deceased. Based on current Michigan case law, both amounts are subject to the single aggregate maximum recovery provided by statute.

In 2013, this combined aggregate maximum amount could not exceed a monthly payment of $5,189. This amount is adjusted each October 1 to reflect changes in the cost of living under rules prescribed by Michigan's Insurance Commission.

Survivor loss benefits are part of PIP benefits, and are payable for up to three years after the decedent's death. The personal representative will have to submit proof of loss of support that would have been received but for the decedent dying. The insurance company's liability to pay this amount may be reduced by other payments the survivor receives, such as workers' compensation benefits or social security survivor benefits. These other monies received by members of the deceased's dependent family act as a set-off to the No-Fault insurer's liability for the economic portion of survivor's loss benefits. A landmark case in Michigan, *Wood v. Auto Owners Insurance Co.,* 469 Mich 401 (2003), laid out the formula for calculating No-Fault survivor loss benefits in light of available set-offs.

In one particular case where I represented the estate, the deceased was a young child, but in terms of emotional ties was the epicenter of the family left behind. There was no economic loss sustained by the loved one's death since the child had no dependents. In this case, I secured the services of a nationally renowned grief expert from New York to help document the loss sustained by the family. I flew the expert to Michigan who met with the family for approximately one week.

The nationally renowned grief expert not only interviewed family members, but also interviewed friends and acquaintances who knew each family member <u>before</u> the death of the deceased, as well as <u>after</u> the death. These collateral contacts helped document the tremendous emotional change in the entire family's life as a result of the death of the child. A 64-page report was generated which documented the emotional devastation that had taken place as a result of the death. This report was shared with the insurance company of the at-fault third party during settlement negotiations. The grief expert also became an expert witness for trial who could, with specificity, now offer testimony on the actual documented grief and mental anguish experienced by family members of the deceased.

These are the types of actions that can be taken by an experienced personal injury attorney to make the claim of the estate much more powerful when it comes to demanding that an insurance company properly compensate surviving family members for the death of a loved one.

The personal representative can also assist the personal injury attorney by participating in a video interview, gathering photos and memorabilia of the deceased, and obtaining records of the accomplishments of the deceased during the deceased's lifetime.

Chapter 2

Obtaining Personal Injury Protection (PIP) Benefits

Personal Injury Protection Benefits

Personal Injury Protection benefits, commonly called PIP benefits, are usually available when injury or death occurs as a result of a motor vehicle accident. *To be deemed a motor vehicle accident at least one of the vehicles involved must have four or more wheels, e.g., a car, truck, or sports vehicle.* For purposes of securing PIP benefits, motorcycle accidents not involving a motorized vehicle with four wheels, do not qualify as a "motor vehicle accident." Trailers, off-road vehicles, even go-karts have been recognized as motor vehicles as long as they have at least four wheels and are registered with Michigan's Secretary of State and are insured.

PIP benefits cover such expenses as wage loss, medical-related expenses, reimbursement for replacement services, home and motor vehicle modification expenses, funeral expenses, and survivor loss benefits.

As a general rule, when representing a client on a third party body injury claim, law firms usually do not have to also represent the client regarding his or her first party claim to recover PIP benefits. An attorney is not usually needed to file claims for first party PIP benefits. Typically, it is something that an individual can file for by following some simple steps.

If, however, you have been injured in a motor vehicle accident and you have problems obtaining your PIP benefits, my firm, or another personal injury firm, can be retained to assist you in obtaining the benefits which you are entitled to receive. In such a case, the client and the attorney representing the client, would enter into a separate retainer agreement, on either an hourly or a contingency basis, to pursue a **breach of contract claim** against the client's own insurance company or the insurance company providing the PIP benefits under the priority rules.

Which insurance company should I contact to receive my PIP benefits?

Under Michigan law, there are **certain rules of priority** that determine which insurance company has the highest priority to pay a motor vehicle accident victim's No-Fault PIP benefits. It needs to be kept in mind, however, that these priority rules are different depending on whether you were an *occupant*, i.e. you were a driver or a passenger, or a *non-occupant*, i.e. you were someone who was injured by a motor vehicle but not riding in a motor vehicle, for example a bicyclist, pedestrian, or someone riding on a motorcycle. Additional priority rules pertain to motorcycle riders since, as stated, Michigan's No-Fault law pertains to accidents involving vehicles with four wheels, as opposed to two.

1. For occupants of a private vehicle, the order of priority is as follows:

a. your own auto insurer;

b. if you have a spouse, and don't have insurance, then your spouse's auto insurer;

c. the auto insurance company of your closest living relative who lives in [domiciled in] the same household that you do;

d. the auto insurer of the owner(s) of the occupied vehicle or registrant(s) (there may be more than one owner or registrant of the vehicle you were "occupying" at the time of the accident);

e. the auto insurer of the operator (the driver) of the occupied vehicle, and if none;

f. the Assigned Claims Fund. The Michigan Assigned Claims Fund is a fund monitored by the Michigan Assigned Claims Facility

(ACF). This facility is a State agency that was created under the No-Fault Act to cover situations when no No-Fault insurance company can be identified to be responsible for paying PIP benefits. The ACF is the last recourse for seriously injured victims of motor vehicle accidents to make sure that they receive PIP benefits in a motor vehicle accident. The Assigned Claims Facility takes victims' claims and assigns them to various insurance companies who have agreed to such assignments by underwriting insurance policies in Michigan; or

g. the occupant of an employer's vehicle.

(There are different rules of priority when it comes to accidents involving **an employer's vehicle.** If you were an occupant of an employer's vehicle and injured in a motor vehicle accident, then you would file your claim for PIP benefits with the employer's insurance company, irrespective of whether the vehicle is owned or registered to your current employer, or the employer of your spouse or a relative.)

2. **For occupants of a public transportation vehicle, e.g., a bus or taxi, the priority is as follows:**
   a. your motor vehicle insurer, and if none;
   b. the motor vehicle insurer of your spouse or relative living under the same roof, and if none;
   c. the bus or taxi insurer, and if none;
   d. the motor vehicle insurer of the driver of the same, and if none;
   e. the Assigned Claims Fund.

3. **For non-occupants (pedestrians, bicyclists, and motorcycle riders) the order of priority is as follows:**
   a. your own auto insurer;
   b. if you have a spouse, and don't have insurance, then your spouse's auto insurer;
   c. if neither you nor a spouse has an auto insurer, then the auto insurer of your closest living relative who lives in the same household that you do;
   d. the auto insurer for the owner(s) or registrant(s) of the vehicle(s) involved in the accident (there may be more than one owner or registrant of a vehicle involved, and more than one vehicle involved in the accident. Under priority rules, each of the owners or

registrants may be equally liable for payment of PIP benefits);

e. the auto insurer of the operators (the drivers) of the motor vehicles that were involved in the accident (there may be more than one driver of more than one vehicle involved); and

f. if coverage isn't available through any of the previously named entities, then you should file your claim with Michigan Assigned Claims Fund.

4. For accidents involving motorcyclists, the order of priority is as follows:

a. the auto insurer of the owner or registrant of the motor vehicle–or vehicles involved in the accident;

b. the auto insurer of the motor vehicle's operators (the driver or drivers), as the case may be;

c. the motor vehicle insurer covering the motorcycle driver;

d. the motor vehicle insurer that covers the motorcycle's owner or registrant; and

e. the Michigan Assigned Claims Fund.

Who is the Vehicle's "Owner"

It needs to be kept in mind that sometimes it is tricky to determine who is defined as the vehicle's "owner." Typically, the owner is the registered title owner according to the records of the Secretary of State. Michigan's No-Fault Act, however, states that a person may be an owner if:

1. the person rents or leases the motor vehicle for more than 30 days;
2. the person holds legal title to the motor vehicle, except when they are in the business of leasing the motor vehicle, and have leased it out for more than 30 days, or:
3. a person has the "immediate right" under an installment sales contract to possess the motor vehicle.

Having an experienced motor vehicle accident attorney to check these issues out can be very helpful since determining ownership in such cases can be extremely difficult, even for a lawyer who regularly handles auto accident cases.

What are the steps to obtain my PIP benefits?

The responsible auto insurance company will provide you with claim forms that you must fill out in order to receive your PIP benefits. Promptly filling out these forms and mailing them back to the insurance company will help ensure, in most cases, that you receive the benefits you are entitled to receive.

What benefits are available?

PIP provides a wide spectrum of benefits that include medical, vocational, and funeral benefits. They are described in more detail below.

Medical

As a general rule, any item or service that a physician recommends as reasonably necessary for your care and recovery is covered as part of your PIP benefits. This includes reimbursement for the cost of all hospital, medical, and chiropractic treatment, together with necessary medical products or devices, such as prosthesis, crutches, a wheelchair, a home hospital bed, etc. Additionally, prescribed physical therapy and vocational rehabilitation are also covered expenses. Travel costs to and from places of treatment are also reimbursable. Therefore, it is extremely important that you keep an accurate record of all medical-related expenses incurred and mileage traveled.

Survivor Loss Benefits When There Has Been a Death

Under survivor loss benefits, benefits for funeral and burial expenses are payable and the amount will be dictated by your insurance policy. As stated earlier, the policy amount may not be less than $1,750 or more than $5,000. Additionally, as stated, under survivor loss benefits, Michigan law requires the insurance company providing PIP benefits to you (usually your own insurance company), to give you money comparable to what you would have received as a dependent from your loved one had they not been killed in an auto accident. Dependents include: spouses, minor children, and physically or mentally incapacitated children (even over 18 years of age) whenever the facts suggest that such an individual was a dependent. Survivor loss benefits also cover the money a dependent would need to obtain the services his or her loved one would have performed for the dependent (replacement services), up to the rate of $20 per day, 7 days a week, for three years after the death of the decedent.

Currently, until October 1, 2014, the total amount payable under this section, as previously stated, cannot exceed the monthly statutory maximum provided under the No-Fault law ($5,282). This amount was set on October 1, 2013, and will be adjusted again on October 1, 2014, and each October 1 thereafter. This amount will be adjusted based on a cost of living factor. This survivor loss No-Fault benefit is payable for three years from the date of the accident.

The amount of No-Fault survivor-loss benefits actually received by dependents will be reduced by setoffs for other benefits received by survivors. Other benefits that reduce wage loss and replacement service expenses include: workers' compensation benefits and social security benefits. There is a complicated formula for determining the impact of these setoffs. This formula was first enunciated in the case of *Wood v. Auto Owners Insurance Company,* 469 Mich 401 (2003). This formula (the *Wood v. Auto Owners* formula) is now relied upon by insurance companies to calculate net survivor loss benefits after allowable setoffs.

Reimbursements for payments to individuals who performed services that would normally have been performed by the injured party are also available for up to three years after the time of the accident.

TIP:

It is important to immediately recognize that from the day of the accident, individuals, frequently family members, can be employed to perform the services that the injured or deceased party previously performed for herself or for her family. Waiting to hire someone to help can jeopardize those benefits as reimbursements are limited to $20 per day, and each day the services are not used, is a day of lost benefits.

Types of Replacement Services

Some examples of replacement services that can be reimbursable include:

- household cleaning (vacuuming, dusting, washing floors, taking out the trash, changing the linen on beds, cleaning bathrooms, etc.)
- doing laundry (folding clothes, ironing, putting clothes away, etc.)
- performing lawn care functions (mowing the grass, raking leaves, weeding, trimming hedges, etc.)
- grocery shopping and shopping for children's clothes
- snow shoveling
- providing for child care
- making household repairs
- making vehicle repairs (changing oil, etc.)
- preparing meals
- bathing family members and caring for the physical needs of other family members

Note: *Expenses for obtaining replacement services must be reasonably incurred. Court decisions have recognized that a simple, oral agreement, or even an implied agreement between family members that they will be compensated is enough. Spouses, children, and parents of an injured party are the norm, rather than the exception, to perform such replacement services. Don't be timid when asking for reimbursement for these expenses. Remember that you paid for these benefits every time you paid your insurance premiums.*

Medically-Related Expenses

Some examples of the medical care and reasonable rehabilitation services that PIP benefits cover include:

- doctor visits
- chiropractic visits
- hospitalizations
- X-rays, MRIs, CT scans, Digital Motion X-rays
- physical therapy treatment
- surgeries
- psychotherapy
- speech therapy
- cognitive therapy
- vocational rehabilitation
- prescription medications
- counseling
- job training and job placement services

Attendant Care

Additionally, in-home attendant care services can be provided to the victim by outside agencies or by a nurse or a family member. Attendant care services may involve bathing, dressing, administering medicine, helping individuals to use the toilet, and just monitoring the individual, including during periods of rest.

Home and Motor Vehicle Modifications

Home modifications, (constructing ramps, widening doors, lowering countertops, or installing elevators etc.) that allow the accident victim to return home despite his or her accident-related injuries, are reimbursable. As are vehicle modifications, (wheelchair accessibility etc.) so that the individual can drive the motor vehicle, despite their accident-related limitations.

Vocational Retraining

The No-Fault law has historically been liberally construed to provide coverage for all types of reasonable expenses necessitated by a claimant's accident-related injury. For obvious reasons, determining what constitutes "reasonable and necessary expenses" has been the subject of much debate. The more serious the injury, the more incidental expenses will be covered, such as nursing home care and special arrangements to properly care for the claimant. Part of rehabilitative benefits can also include vocational and occupational rehabilitation. Insurance companies like to do everything possible to try and get someone who is not able to work because of an injury back to some form of work to reduce their company's wage loss responsibility. Take note however, this incentive <u>ends</u> near the three year limitation for the insurance company to pay for work loss.

More than one Michigan case has held that reasonable expenses necessary for vocational rehabilitation are allowable expenses within the No-Fault Act. In cases where a claimant's injuries have left the claimant physically able to perform only sedentary work, the court has held that tuition, and room and board costs may be reasonably necessary to provide the claimant with a vocation that allows for sedentary employment. In such a case, when the claimant's education is done, it allows the claimant to return to work and receive a salary that was at or even greater than the one he or she had earned before the accident.

Guardianship/Conservatorship Fees

For catastrophically injured persons, guardianship and/or conservatorship (including the legal fees and court costs incurred to establish the same) are also reimbursable for accident victims who have become legally incapacitated. In cases where there are long-term permanently debilitating injuries, such as in the case of a closed head injury, case manager or case management cost may also be reimbursable when necessary to assist with the individual's medical regimen.

How do I qualify to receive no-fault PIP benefits?

It's important to keep in mind that if you are injured in a motor vehicle accident, how you were injured is irrelevant as to whether you are entitled to No-Fault PIP benefits. That is where the name "No-Fault Insurance" comes from. Personal Injury Protection benefits are due to an injured party without regard to fault.

To qualify for No-Fault PIP benefits, an accident victim, or his or her estate, must satisfy the following five facts:

1. a motor vehicle (four or more wheels) was involved in the accident;
2. the accident caused body injury or death to the party or the estate seeking PIP benefits;
3. the injury or death was the result of accidental rather than intentional conduct;
4. the motor vehicle involved in the accident was being operated, (driven), maintained, or used as a motor vehicle during the time of the accident; and
5. the accidental body injury or death arose out of the operation, maintenance, or use of the motor vehicle as a motor vehicle.

If all of the five requirements above can be proven, then the benefit that you are seeking to obtain must be one of the benefits covered under the No-Fault Act: reimbursement for medical-related expenses, reimbursement for wage loss, reimbursement for the cost of hiring someone to perform replacement services for you, or survivorship loss benefits.

The One Year Back Rule

There is a one year statute of limitations on payment of all No-Fault benefits. This basically means that you lose your right to be reimbursed by the responsible insurance company for any expense or benefit if it is not paid by the insurance company within one year after the expense is incurred or the benefit is due. The one year statute of limitations is automatically tolled or stopped when a lawsuit is filed against the insurance company for the wrongful non-payment of the benefit.

If the insurance company fails or refuses to pay a benefit or expense, *insist that a letter be sent **to you** explaining specifically why the benefit is being denied.* Document all of your contacts with the adjuster. Keep duplicate copies of your correspondence with the adjuster to serve as verification of your requests for reimbursement and to document the timeliness of your request(s). If you do not resolve your claim within 90 days, I strongly recommend that you contact an attorney and schedule an appointment. Do not sit on your rights. Waiting can cause you to lose your right to be reimbursed for medical expenses, lost wages, replacement services, and other PIP benefits that you are entitled to receive.

Timeliness of Your Reimbursement

An insurance company is required to reimburse you for a well-documented expense that you have incurred, and that is covered by your PIP benefits, within 30 days after you have submitted the claim. If provided, it is important to use the specific forms sent by your insurance company. And, fill them out *in detail* for the reimbursements you are seeking.

If not paid within 30 days, such an unpaid claim can be deemed to be unreasonably denied unless the insurance company has made a legitimate request for verification of the expense and you have failed to provide it. After 30 days of supplying proper documentation for reimbursement, the insurance company can be liable for any attorney fees incurred in having to obtain payment for such expenses. This is usually, however, a very difficult payment to receive.

For this reason, it is strongly suggested that you contact an attorney as soon as possible if you are having difficulty obtaining reimbursement for expenses that should be covered by your insurance company. To preserve the right to receive reimbursement for these expenses a lawsuit must be filed prior to one year from the time that the expense was incurred. Therefore, waiting to contact an attorney until 10 or 11 months after the bill was incurred will put reimbursement for the full expense in jeopardy.

Suggestions for Handling Your Own No-Fault Claim

Submit an Application for No-Fault Benefits to your insurance company as soon as possible following the accident. You need to notify your own insurance company no later than one year following the accident. Contact your insurance agent for an application for PIP benefits. Generally, most PIP benefits that you will be seeking will be for wage loss and/or replacement services. If you do not have your own motor vehicle insurance and you were a pedestrian or a passenger injured in a motor vehicle accident, you should contact an attorney to help determine the appropriate insurance company from which to request an Application for No-Fault Benefits. The priority has been discussed in this book, yet my experience is that you may have difficulty figuring out the priority on your own.

Any time you are involved in a motor vehicle accident, it is important to notify your PIP carrier (usually your own motor vehicle insurance company), about the fact that you were involved in a motor vehicle accident. If you wait too long to notify your own insurance company, your own insurance policy may dictate that you are prohibited from receiving benefits. Keep in mind that you may not believe that you have any injuries to report. Nevertheless, as time elapses, problems may develop, even years later, and if you haven't notified your insurance company within one year from the date of the accident, you will likely be barred from seeking any type of a recovery.

Within 30 days of submitting your application to an insurance company you should receive a letter from the No-Fault carrier advising you of your claim number, the name of the claims adjuster handling your file, and the address of the office where your claim is being administered. This is the information that you need to provide to your doctors, physical therapists, speech therapists, etc. for billing purposes.

It is very important to establish and maintain an open line of communication with your claims adjuster. Provide any information that he or she requests as soon as you reasonably can. Contact your adjuster directly if your medical bills are not being paid on time, or your wage loss reimbursement check is not arriving when it should. Additionally, do not be afraid to contact your claims adjuster if you have any questions at all regarding your claim. I always suggest putting in writing that you would like to know what possible benefits you may be entitled to receive based on the unique facts of your injury.

If you are entitled to wage loss benefits, ask your adjuster if the benefits will be paid weekly, bi-weekly, or monthly, and then budget your money accordingly. Again, use the forms provided by your adjuster to submit the request for reimbursement for mileage, prescriptions and replacement services. Use certified mail to submit these forms to your adjuster on a regular basis. Keep a photocopy of the forms you have submitted.

Independent Medical Exam (IME): Could be trouble...

I choose to call these evaluations *insurance* medical exams rather than *independent* medical exams. Whenever an adjuster has scheduled you for an IME, trouble is on the horizon. That said, if your adjuster schedules you for an independent medical examination (IME), *you must attend* this evaluation. If you do not attend an IME, you will jeopardize your PIP benefits.

The following are my recommendations for handling an IME appointment:

- I suggest that you immediately contact a personal injury attorney to discuss your participation in an IME.
- Take an ally with you into the examination room. And both of you pay particular attention to what the doctor does, or more importantly, what the doctor does not do during the examination.

- Time how long you were examined by the doctor, as often these "examinations" take place at record speed—maybe ten minutes!
- Make sure to ask for mileage reimbursement from your PIP insurance company in advance of attending an IME.
- Reject having someone from the insurance company transport you as the individual transporting you is typically told to ask you questions about your injuries and then to report your responses back to your carrier.
- When you are attending an IME, do not discuss anything except your medical condition. Keep in mind that when you attend an IME, your actions in the lobby and coming and going to the examination are often scrutinized by individuals at the IME office. It's amazing how things that were said nonchalantly to individuals at the doctor's office end up in the IME report. Staff observations such as "the patient had no problems ambulating in the parking lot and walking into the waiting room" can be found in an IME report.

Hiring an Independent Case Manager or Taking Advantage of Case Manager Services Provided by Your Physician or your Physician's Clinic

Some physicians and/or clinics or hospital retain the services of a case manager to help ensure that both the injured party and the physicians who are providing services receive the compensation and benefits due to them. Frequently, the services of a case manager will be reimbursed by your insurance company. Speak with your treating doctor about possible options; perhaps he or she will be able to write a "prescription" saying you need the services of a case manager to assist you in securing your PIP benefits. Be sure your case manager is proactive about seeking reimbursement for your lost wages and household or vehicle modification expenses, and placement services and/or reimbursement for family members who might be providing attendant care services—you can be pretty confident the case manager will be attentive to the reimbursement needs of your physician and the hospital and/or clinic. Having an advocate to make sure that you receive all of the benefits you are entitled to can make a huge difference in the quality of life that you will lead after a motor vehicle accident. An important fact to keep in mind is that these benefits are not being *given to you* as charity—they are benefits that you paid for, in advance, should you be injured in a motor vehicle accident. You paid for these benefits each and every time you paid your insurance premium!

There are also independent individuals, perhaps a registered nurse with additional expertise in this area for example, who can also act as case managers. These individuals, however, must be hired by you. While that may seem like a financial burden, if the injured party is suffering from a catastrophic injury, the case manager's advocacy and inside knowledge may be able to provide invaluable assistance in assuring that the injured party receives everything he or she is entitled to. You can ask your attorney for a referral or a recommendation.

No-Fault benefits are based on your contract with your insurance company, and you are entitled to receive benefits as part of Michigan's No-Fault law, which all insurance companies are required to follow. Therefore, you need never apologize for seeking all of the benefits you are entitled to receive by virtue of the contract you entered into with your insurance company under Michigan's No-Fault law.

A First Party Claim

If you are not receiving benefits you are entitled to receive either by law or from your own insurance carrier (or the insurance carrier assigned to you under the priority rules discussed earlier), then you have a *first party claim*.

A *first party claim* is for a "breach of contract" rather than a tort claim (for negligence). If your wage loss claim has been denied, and your insurance adjuster has denied your wage loss claim, you need to contact an attorney familiar with handling first party claims. That attorney can file a breach of contract lawsuit against your own insurance company or the PIP carrier assigned to you under the priority rules. The same applies if your PIP insurance company refuses to pay for chiropractic care or physical therapy appointments. Often, insurance companies hire one of their regular IME doctors to perform a ten minute examination on you only to determine that you have reached MMI (maximum medical improvement), a phrase coined by the insurance industry. If an adjuster or one of their IME doctors has determined that you have reached your MMI and further physical therapy or medical treatment care is unnecessary, they will attempt to *close* your medical file, and leave you out in the cold, so to speak, for reimbursements for further medical expenses.

If such a denial occurs, you should immediately contact a personal injury attorney familiar with handling first party claims. Typically, they will take your case on a contingency basis, although they may also agree to perform services on an hourly basis. They may also give you advice to allow you to handle your own case without any need to hire a lawyer.

It needs to be kept in mind that in cases dealing with reimbursement for medical expenses, especially for attendant care expenses for those persons needing 24 hour care, the dollar amount of such first-party claims can be staggering. Obtaining the PIP benefits you are entitled to receive under your own insurance policy or under Michigan's No-Fault Law can make all the difference in the quality of life that you or a loved one leads after being injured in a motor vehicle accident.

Third Party Claims

Recovering Compensation for Serious Injuries,
A Serious Permanent Disfigurement, and/or
A Wrongful Death Caused By an At-Fault Driver

Several concepts must be kept in mind when considering your options to pursue a third party claim against the responsible third party who caused your injuries in a motor vehicle accident or who caused the death of your loved one:

1. Statute of limitations.

In Michigan, there is a statute of limitations that states that you have only three years from the date of your motor vehicle accident to institute a lawsuit against the responsible driver who caused your injuries or the death of your loved one. If you don't obtain compensation for your injuries (your lost wages above and beyond what your PIP benefits covered) and compensation for your non-economic losses (your pain and suffering, depression, mental anguish), then you must file a lawsuit, which tolls (stops) the statute of limitations, before three years from the date of your motor vehicle accident. Failure to file your lawsuit before the expiration of the three year limitation period bars you from pursuing a third party claim against the third party (and their insurance company), who caused your injuries, or the death of your loved one.

If you are representing the estate of a loved one who died in a motor vehicle accident, the time for filing a law suit may be extended by opening an estate and issuing Letters of Authority. These actions, however, must take place prior to three years from the date of the decedent's motor vehicle accident. Make sure to check with an experienced motor vehicle accident attorney to see if the extension will apply.

2. *Document your third party claim.*

Most third party claims, <u>can,</u> if properly documented, be resolved without filing a lawsuit. For this reason, in most cases, it is imperative that you seek the advice of an experienced motor vehicle accident attorney <u>well in advance</u> of the expiration of the three year statute of limitations. That being said, I have had clients who have contacted me within two weeks of the statute of limitations deadline, seeking a second opinion as to whether they have a case.

On more than one occasion, I have actually filed a lawsuit only days before a statute of limitations has expired to protect my client's ability to obtain justice and to be compensated for their damages. I have done this while I have continued to evaluate their claim. Fortunately, in all of those cases, I have been able to determine that they did have a third party case, and have actually settled more than one case for hundreds of thousands of dollars. Keep in mind, had the client just waited a week or two longer, there would have been no recovery possible. That being said, waiting until the statute of limitations is about to expire is clearly *not* the way to go as it places undo stress on all parties involved.

3. *How the claims process actually works.*

Documentation is the key. Once a party's loss has been sufficiently documented, the personal injury attorney representing you will typically make a *demand* on the responsible insurance company that insured the third party who caused your accident. In most cases, the lawyer representing you will deal with an adjuster working for the insurance company to see if a mutual agreement can be reached on the value of your third party claim. This value is known as a *settlement value* and means that both parties are likely going to have to compromise on what they think the value of the claim is worth in order to settle the matter without litigation.

Sometimes reasonable people can differ, and a lawsuit will have to be filed. On the other hand, claims adjusters have a job to do: adjust and finalize a claim in a fashion that protects the insurance company they represent. Protecting the insurance company includes paying a reasonable amount of money to compensate an injured party since that is the purpose of insurance in the first place. But, it also includes not paying significantly more than the claim is worth. Paying more or less than a claim is worth is a subjective standard, meaning that reasonable minds can differ on what is a fair amount to settle a case.

4. What's the value of my case?

I am often asked by clients "How much is my case worth?" I tell clients that it is virtually impossible to predict the value of their case until all of the information has been collected and we know the nature and extent of the client's recovery from their injury. Obviously, this is different in a death case, but it still takes time to develop the full nature and extent of the grieving party's losses. When evaluating injury cases, there are many factors that determine the value of an individual case. Such factors include:

- The actual amount of all medical bills.
- How the medical bills were incurred— diagnostic tests, treatments, physical therapy, hospital stays, prescription medication, over-the-counter medication, chiropractic care, and other treatment.
- How much income and other employment benefits were lost as a result of the injury. This would include lost pay, sick leave, vacation time, loss of insurance benefits, and other losses resulting from the injury.
- The actual extent of the injury and how it affected the daily life of the injured party. This would include limits on household activities, sports and leisure activities, and social life.
- Whether any aspect of the party's injuries is permanent. This would include permanent disfigurement such as scars, blemishes, and other disfiguring characteristics.
- Whether any of the injuries required prolonged hospitalization.
- The extent of liability on the part of the potential defendant. For example, was the defendant a drunk driver?
- Whether there is any evidence that the injured party or deceased party was partly at-fault for causing the accident.

- The status of the law as it relates to each individual case at the time that the case is being evaluated. Courts continue to make new decisions determining whether an injured party has suffered a threshold injury. When the case is being evaluated for settlement purposes, we need to deeply consider whether we are dealing with an injury that borders on being classified as seriously affecting the person's ability to lead a normal life.

- The quality of the witnesses, including those witnesses who will testify about the accident, the injuries sustained, and the medical treatment provided.

- Other factors such as the amount of pain, suffering, inconvenience, and loss of consortium (how the injury has affected the marital relationship of the injured party, both emotionally and physically).

- Which insurance company is involved in adjusting the case. Some insurance companies are more reasonable than others.

- In which county would your case be tried should it have to go before a jury to be resolved. The insurance carriers know which counties tend to return higher or lower verdicts in personal injury cases.

The above list is just a few of the factors that must be taken into consideration by an experienced motor vehicle accident attorney in determining the settlement value of a case. Some factors are more important than others, and because insurance companies require specific documentation, it is the responsibility of the injured party, the personal representative of a deceased party, and the attorney representing your third party claim, to provide the insurance company with as much clear information as possible to support your claim when trying to reach a settlement.

5. *Settling your third party claim.*

In determining the *settlement value*, the injured party needs to keep in mind that the longer the claim goes without being adjusted, the more stress is placed on the injured party since the injured party typically wants their claim to be finalized as soon as possible. The longer a claim remains un resolved also means that the settlement proceeds are not in the injured party's bank account earning interest (rather than in the insurance company's bank account).

From the insurance company's point of view, when a demand is first made for a payment to the injured party, the insurance company places a reserve on the insurance company's assets in an amount deemed to be of sufficient value to adjust the claim. Typically, insurance adjusters look at policy limits as one of the factors when making the decision of how much money to put in reserve to adjust the claim. On top of policy limits, however, the insurance company must also look at their costs for their own legal counsel if the case has to be litigated, together with any out-of-pocket expenses such as conducting depositions, hiring experts, etc.

The same factors need to be kept in mind by the injured party. If the matter is litigated, the injured party will likely incur additional legal expenses by conducting depositions of experts, paying expert witness fees, paying transcript fees, and paying for court costs.

When an injured party's personal injury attorney makes a *demand*, it is a formal expression. The insurance company will typically advise an injured party's lawyer "send us your demand." Using the word "demand" isn't meant to be rude or offensive. You are not demanding that you be paid a certain amount of money. Rather, making *a demand* refers to the sum of money that you are requesting to compensate you fully and fairly for the losses you have sustained as a result of the motor vehicle accident in which you were injured, perhaps including serious permanent disfigurement.

In a demand, your attorney will document lost wages **and if, and only if,** your injury reaches a threshold level of causing a serious impairment of a body function or serious permanent scarring, then your attorney will outline how your injuries will have an impact on non-economic damages.

As of this writing, a serious impairment of a body function means an objectively manifested impairment of an important body function that affects the injured party's general ability to lead his or her normal life. An impairment of a body function does not have to be permanent in order to be a serious impairment of a body function, however, it does need to be objectively manifested. There needs to be a medically identifiable injury or condition that has a physical basis. It is not enough for an injured party to state: "I just hurt all over."

Some medical documentation is required to objectively point to why an injured party is experiencing his pain and suffering. Although there are some general diagnoses such as fibromyalgia, which have to do with an injured party's overall physical state without being able to specifically identify the cause of the party's condition, generally speaking, juries are looking for muscle spasms, damaged tissue or bones, etc., that are able to be documented by a medical test such as X-rays, MRIs, CT scans, Digital Motion X-rays, PET scans, and the like.

Non-economic damages include pain and suffering that you have incurred and will likely incur in the future. Non-economic damages also include compensation for mental anguish, fright, shock, denial of social pleasure and enjoyments, embarrassment, humiliation, or mortification.

All forms of non-economic damages are also allowed for future pain and suffering if reasonable certainty of such pain and suffering is proven. Depending on the nature and extent of the injuries suffered by you, juries can be asked to consider shame, mortification, mental pain, and anxiety that you have had to endure. Annoyance, discomfort, and humiliation related to physical injuries are also proper damage elements for the jury to consider. Severe cases of depression are also compensable if directly related to the injuries you have received.

Assuming that your personal injury attorney has been able to document your injuries and is satisfied that your injuries have reached a point where your lawyer is able to define the nature and extent of your injuries, then the documentation is put together and sent to an insurance adjuster representing the third party who caused the accident.

Such documentation can include videos taken of you and other loved ones of the injured or deceased. Your attorney will do his or her best to fully document the nature and extent of how much damage has been done to you and to the loved ones of a deceased as a result of an accident. Such documentation can include providing copies of medical, employment, physical therapy, and counseling records. Expert opinions by vocational rehabilitation experts may also document the bleak outlook to be expected for any future employment available to a severely injured party.

Early on when you retain an attorney to represent you, your attorney will notify the other driver that you are pursuing a claim for recovery of your injuries, and will also request that the other driver notify his or her own insurance company of your pending claim. In most cases, the other driver will then promptly notify his or her own insurance company of the fact that you are represented by an attorney and that you are pursuing a third party claim. Within a very short time, an insurance company representing the third party will have an adjuster assigned to handle your third party claim, and he or she will communicate with your lawyer identifying the third party claim number, and request that all future correspondence be directed to that adjuster.

Your demand will be sent to that adjuster when you make your claim for compensation for your injuries. Typically, after sending the demand to the third party adjuster, there is a time period where your attorney will see if it is possible to obtain a "meeting of the minds" between your attorney and the claims adjuster of the third party driver as to the value of your claim. The time period for negotiations to occur could be as short as 30 to 60 days, or it could go on for six months or more. How long such negotiations continue depends largely on whether your attorney believes that *good faith* negotiations are taking place.

When evaluating whether good faith negotiations are occurring, your attorney will determine whether the parties are far apart in the settlement value being placed on your claim, whether there are multiple players involved, and whether other information is being sought to document one side's position. All of these factors may support continuing the negotiation process to determine if a good faith settlement can be reached without having to litigate the value of your claim.

On more than one occasion I have settled claims for clients for one million dollars or more without ever filing a lawsuit. But, such settlements do not occur without a significant amount of time and effort documenting why such a significant amount is justified to adjust a client's claim. Most of the time, my clients do not want to file a lawsuit. So my clients typically are very pleased to obtain a large settlement without having to sue an at-fault party.

There are some motor vehicle accident attorneys who believe that obtaining fair compensation values can only be obtained after filing a lawsuit. I am not one of those attorneys. As of the writing of this book I have tried 334 jury trials in my career and I've only lost three—the majority of these trials were when I was a prosecuting attorney. I am not afraid to try a lawsuit. In fact, I enjoy being in the courtroom before juries, *it is my clients* who do not like to go to court and who wish, in most cases, to avoid litigation, and I try to respect that whenever possible.

There are exceptions. For instance, when a family has lost a loved one as a result of a senseless motor vehicle accident—as a result of drunk driving for example. Sometimes they may want to sue the responsible driver to hold them fully accountable for their loved one's death. But even in these cases, having to go through a trial where all of the emotions of losing their loved one have to be publically dredged up is something that most clients find overwhelming.

The question of whether to file a lawsuit usually comes down to whether the insurance company adjusting the claim is willing to fully and fairly compensate an injured party for their loss. That injured party could be the estate of the person killed in a motor vehicle accident, which would include all of those who have suffered a loss–spouse, children, parents, grandparents, and siblings of the deceased. The injured party could also be a person who survived the accident and that injured person's claim would include the person's spouse and minor children who might also be affected by any economic loss of a wage earner's support.

If an insurance company is not willing to offer a settlement figure which fairly takes into consideration the losses sustained by all of those affected by the motor vehicle accident, then the attorney representing the injured party and/or the injured parties estate, *must be willing to litigate the matter.* When the insurance company involved is adjusting the claim, it is fair for them, as it is fair for the injured party and the clients the attorney represents, to take into consideration the financial cost of litigation, as well as the emotional cost of litigation on all parties.

It is also fair for both the insurance company and the client and his or her attorney to take into consideration that a jury could award more or less for a claim. It is also fair for both sides to consider the time-price differential involved. The offer to pay a certain amount of money <u>now</u>, is worth more than paying the same amount of money a year from now when the claim is finally presented to a jury (or resolved along the way during litigation). The longer the insurance company has that same amount of money to invest, rather than paying that same amount to the injured party and/or to the estate of a deceased party, is a consideration for both sides (especially considering additional expenses to be incurred during the litigation process).

So, while your attorney attempts to determine the wisdom of continuing the negotiation process, you need to keep in contact with your attorney to evaluate the seriousness of the good faith efforts to resolve your claim.

During this time, it is important to listen to your attorney as he or she advises you about the nature of the negotiations taking place, and whether he or she believes that it will be possible to resolve and settle your claim without litigation. Make sure to promptly return all phone calls, emails, and communications from your attorney and his or her staff. Your prompt responses will assist them so they can respond quickly to any issues that arise during the settlement process and better serve you.

Approximately 90% of third party claims are resolved during this negotiation process. Sometimes parties engage in facilitation efforts in which you and your attorney meet with the third party claims adjuster, and possibly the attorney representing the at-fault driver, and determine if a settlement can be reached (<u>even</u> before a lawsuit has been filed).

The process of trying to facilitate a settlement will only be undertaken by your attorney if he or she believes that there is a realistic possibility of resolving your third party claim without litigating the same. If your attorney believes that you and the insurance company's adjuster are too far apart, he or she may recommend litigation. This happens in about 10% of the cases.

The lawsuit will usually be brought against the person, persons, or company, who caused your injuries, or the death of your loved one and not against the insurance company unless the case involves an uninsured or underinsured motorist case.

In some cases, your attorney may suggest waiting a period of time before commencing the lawsuit in hopes that the insurance company will increase its evaluation of the value of your claim. This could also occur if the attorney is waiting to determine whether you are able to become re-employed in another vocation or whether your injuries are going to continue to cause additional physical problems. In cases where parties are significantly far apart with respect to the value of the case, however, litigation is usually necessary.

What factors prompt litigation?

There are several reasons why a case may not settle during the negotiation process. They include:

- The insurance adjuster representing the insurance company of the "at-fault" driver believes that you and your lawyer have requested more compensation than they are voluntarily willing to pay to adjust your claim.

- The responsibility for causing your injuries or the death of your loved one is being contested by the adjuster for the insurance company or the adjuster for the insurance company believes that you and/or some other party bear some of the responsibility for causing your own injuries or the death of your loved one.

- The insurance company is stalling for time to determine whether you and your attorney will reduce how much money you are requesting to adjust the claim or to determine whether you will file a lawsuit.

- The insurance company, because of certain policy reasons, has decided to resist payment of claims of the type that you or your estate are maintaining and has decided to force you to go through a lawsuit rather than making any attempt to adjust your claim.

- The adjuster for the insurance company does not believe that you were injured, or that your injuries reached a threshold level and therefore, the insurance company may have no responsibility to pay your claim. Accordingly, the company is, in fact, denying your claim, requiring you to pursue a lawsuit to prove your entitlement to compensation.

- If settlement negotiations have determined that a lawsuit must be filed, your attorney will explain in detail what you will have to do in the process. The process begins with filing court papers in the court where your claim will be adjudicated. This is typically in the county where the motor vehicle accident occurred. The lawsuit is usually filed in the circuit court for such county since the value of your claim will typically exceed $25,000.

Filing A Lawsuit

The litigation process has the
following steps:

1. Your lawyer will prepare a summons and complaint.
The summons and complaint outline how the
accident occurred and the general nature and extent
of the injuries that you, your spouse, and/or your
minor children, the estate of your loved one, and/or
your loved one's next-of-kin have suffered as a result
of the motor vehicle accident.

2. The summons and complaint are then served upon
the person, persons, or company who caused the
motor vehicle accident. The responsible at-fault
party(s) is referred to as the defendant, or the
defendants, as the case may be. You and/or the estate
of your loved one are referred to as the plaintiff(s).

3. After the defendant(s) is served with the complaint,
the insurance company representing the defendant(s)
will hire a lawyer to defend the lawsuit and the lawyer
will file an answer to the complaint. The answer to
the complaint typically denies responsibility for the
injuries and/or the death, and may also possibly seek
to bring in other third party defendants who might

have been involved in causing the accident which caused your loss.

4. Thereafter, a process referred to as *discovery* commences during which both sides seek information from the other. You will be involved in this process. The process includes some or all of the following:

- Responding to written questions referred to as interrogatories. Your responses need to be in writing and under oath.
- Offering oral testimony from you, other parties, and witnesses in what are called depositions.
- Oral testimony typically takes place in conference rooms where lawyers are present and a court reporter takes down the questions and answers, and then prepares a written transcript of the oral testimony.
- Submitting and/or responding to requests for documents in which the lawyers request medical reports, witness statements, medical bills, and other documents related to your case. In most cases, your attorney will have to send such documents to the other attorney even if they have already been previously supplied to the insurance company.
- Responding to requests for admissions. This is a process that is available to parties to

attempt to narrow the issues by requiring the other side to admit certain facts that are not in dispute.

5. Trial preparation. This can include taking video depositions of your physicians, meeting with witnesses, filing motions limiting the evidence, and filing trial briefs.

Facilitation

It is typical for both sides to engage in a process known as facilitation, which is an attempt during litigation to settle your case prior to actually going to trial. After the process of discovery has given both sides a greater insight into the merits of each party's position, often the parties are willing to sit down with a third party who is familiar with adjusting motor vehicle claims. This third party is typically an attorney who has handled motor vehicle litigation and knows the strengths and weaknesses of both sides. This third party will attempt to facilitate a settlement by pointing out the strengths and weaknesses of each party's respective case to the other.

This facilitation process is usually done at a lawyer's office. At the lawyer's office, both parties and their attorneys appear and representatives from the defendant's insurance companies also appear. The facilitator goes back and forth between conference rooms where the strengths of each side's position are discussed and encouragement is made to each side to move closer to the other side's position to see if the claim can be resolved.

Some facilitators start the process by allowing each side to present their respective position to the other in a conference room setting. Other facilitators use different approaches to try to bring the parties together. The goal of the facilitator is to reach a settlement in which both sides believe that some of the respective merits of their position have been recognized. This facilitation process is not binding on either party and the discussions that take place are inadmissible in court if the facilitation process is unsuccessful.

Case Evaluation

Case evaluation is a process provided for by court rule in every litigated motor vehicle case. Case evaluation may either take place before or after the facilitation process. In some cases, both sides choose not to facilitate the case, but in every case, the court orders that the value of a plaintiff's claim be reviewed by a case evaluation panel typically made up of three lawyers.

In case evaluation, both the defendant and the plaintiff submit a summary of the issues involved for the case evaluators to review. Typically, this summary includes a discussion of liability, the nature and extent of the injuries, the loss that has occurred, and how such loss or injury has affected the lives of the parties making the claim. In the case of a serious injury, numerous medical records may be included in the case summary. In the case of the death of a loved one, a recitation of facts as to the loss of economic support; a projection of future wage loss; and the loss of the love, society, and companionship of the deceased with his or her next of kin will also be included in the plaintiff's case summary.

After the summaries have been prepared and submitted to the case evaluation panel, a meeting takes place with the evaluation panel, usually at the courthouse. This meeting typically lasts for approximately one hour. At the meeting there will be one attorney who regularly practices representing injured parties, one attorney who regularly practices in representing defendants ("at-fault" drivers and their insurance companies), and a third attorney who is deemed to be *neutral*, who does not regularly represent injured parties or insurance companies.

The three attorneys listen to short oral presentations made by the attorney representing the plaintiff and the attorney representing the defendant or defendants. Questions are sometimes put to each side and depending on the make-up of the particular panel, questions may also be put forth regarding the possibly of each side reaching a settlement within insurance policy limits.

The injured party or next-of-kin, as the case may be, usually do not appear at these evaluation hearings. Sometimes a plaintiff's lawyer may bring a plaintiff to the case evaluation for the limited purpose of allowing the case evaluators to be first-hand witnesses to the disfigurement of an injured party. If this occurs, the injured party usually says nothing and just shows the case evaluators his or her scarring on their body.

Thereafter, the case evaluators meet in private and place a monetary value on the plaintiff's claim. If all case evaluators agree on the value of the case and render a unanimous value, then *that amount* becomes an important case evaluation amount for both sides to consider.

A unanimous case evaluation figure means that if one party rejects this value, the rejecting party must improve their position by more than 10% at trial. Determining this 10% is a bit complicated, and for the sake of this book, suffice it to say your attorney will explain this to you during the litigation process. But if the party rejecting a unanimous case evaluation figure does not improve their position by at least 10%, they will be responsible for the other side's reasonable and actual attorney fees incurred after the rejection of the case evaluation amount.

If the case evaluation award was not unanimous, then the attorney fee sanction does not apply. The potential to have to pay the other side's reasonable and actual attorney fees after a party rejects a unanimous case evaluation award does, in some cases, play a significant role in helping the parties to resolve their claim. Insurance companies usually can afford attorney fee sanctions, while individual litigants may worry more about this possible sanction. Nevertheless, it is a factor to be considered by both sides.

More importantly, however, case evaluation lets both sides know what three experienced attorneys, sitting as case evaluators, believe that the case is worth, in terms of settling the claim prior to a trial. Some case evaluators place a settlement value on a claim rather than a trial value, while other case evaluators legitimately place a value on what they think a jury would likely return.

Deferring to your attorney to evaluate the panel's award, in terms of accepting or rejecting the award, is something that needs careful attention. Even if the case evaluation was not unanimous, both sides can nevertheless still agree to accept the case evaluation number to resolve the plaintiff's claim.

Keep in mind that negotiations on your claim can still continue right up until the time a jury returns a verdict. Many a case has settled on "the doorsteps" of the courthouse- some even while the jury is deliberating! Again, keep in mind that most cases settle during the lawsuit process, while only a small minority of cases actually go all the way to a jury verdict (less than 10%).

How long will the litigation process take?

Keep in mind, that every county has a different number of cases that are on the courts' trial docket. The number of cases awaiting resolution may determine how long your case takes to come to trial.

As discussed, after a complaint has been filed and served on the defendant or defendants, there is a waiting period to allow the defendant(s) to answer the complaint. This time is 21 days, if personally served, or 28 days, if served by mail. If interrogatories have been attached to your complaint then the time for responding is 42 days. It is not unusual for the defendant(s) and his or her attorney (typically hired by their insurance company) to request a short extension of time in order to properly respond to the allegations set forth in your complaint.

After the answer has been filed and initial interrogatories answered, the period of discovery usually takes anywhere from three to six months to complete.

After discovery has been completed, the facilitation or case evaluation process takes place. Thereafter, the court requires the parties to attend a settlement conference if they have not been able to settle the case. A trial date may have been set earlier, or may be set at the settlement conference. Some counties wait to see if the case evaluation process has resolved the case before setting a trial date.

In either event, the trial court judge will typically ask the attorneys if settlement appears likely, and if it does not, how many days will be necessary to properly try the case. The court will want to know how many witnesses are likely to be called and whether the parties believe there is any chance of settling the case rather than actually having a trial. If both attorneys believe that a trial will actually be necessary, the court wants to set aside enough days so that the trial can be tried all at once, rather than spread over a period of time.

As such, the availability on the courts' schedule to try a two, three, or five day jury trial will often dictate when the case is actually scheduled to go to trial. Furthermore, criminal cases typically take precedence over civil cases. It may be two or three months before your case comes before a jury.

Preparing *You* for a Trial

If your case looks like it will be tried before a jury, your attorney will spend a significant amount of time preparing you for what to expect at trial. Often you will have an opportunity to look at videos discussing how to properly respond to questions at your trial.

The attorney representing you will typically spend several hours with you, days in advance of the trial, explaining to you how the process will work, and how you can best present yourself.

Your attorney will talk to you about the jury selection process called *voir dire*. You will also learn about the opening statements that will be made by each side, direct examination questions you are likely to have to respond to, and how to respond to questions asked of you on cross examination by the other side. Your lawyer will explain to you the evidence that will be introduced during the trial and how to best respond to anticipated issues that will arise during the trial. After both sides have presented all of their evidence, they will make a closing argument to the jury, and then the judge will instruct the jury as to the law. The jury will then deliberate and return their verdict. Unlike a criminal case, a verdict will be determined by a decision reached by only five out of the six jurors.

Your attorney will advise you of all of the things that you should do, and just as importantly, the things you should not do on your day in court. Typically, your attorney will advise you of how to dress, what questions are likely to be asked, how to act during the trial to best convey to the jury the seriousness of your claim, and how to convey to jurors that this is your one opportunity to obtain justice for your injuries and losses, and to receive full, fair, and complete compensation for the losses you've sustained.

Again, it needs to be kept in mind that many personal injury claims are settled without the need for litigation (approximately 90%) and of those claims that actually do enter into the litigation process, an additional 90% of those litigated claims settle without having an actual jury verdict returned. But, what is important for the consumer to understand is that obtaining the advice and help of an experienced motor vehicle accident attorney who regularly tries case in court and obtains substantial verdicts is extremely important to having your claim receive the value that it should, since the insurance companies know who is and who is not willing to actually try cases to a verdict.

Having your motor vehicle accident claim handled by an attorney who is not well-respected by defense attorneys will lessen the value of your claim. It is also important that you be comfortable with the attorney you select. You will spend a significant amount of time with that attorney if your claim is to be properly compensated. Usually, having an attorney that is well-respected in the local area where your case will be tried also results in obtaining a better settlement of your claim.

Chapter 4

Do I Need To Hire A Motor Vehicle Accident Attorney

Should I Seek Help to Receive The Compensation and Benefits I Am Entitled To Under Michigan's No-Fault Law? If so, how much will it cost me?

Questions and Answers Regarding Hiring an Attorney

Question: When I have been injured, do I need an attorney to help me recover compensation or benefits under Michigan's No-Fault law?

Answer: If you have been injured, the first question that needs to be asked is: How serious are your injuries? If your injuries are minimal and/or will not cause a permanent serious disfigurement of a portion of your body, then your injuries may not justify hiring an attorney. If your first party claims adjuster is providing you with your PIP benefits (wage loss, reimbursement for replacement services, etc.), then you may not need to hire an attorney to assist you in securing your PIP benefits. Nevertheless, I typically suggest that you at least confer with a motor vehicle accident attorney to make sure that you receive all the benefits you are entitled to receive from your first party insurance carrier.

If you have been seriously injured, such that one of your important body functions has been impaired or you have received a serious, permanent disfigurement of a portion of your body, it is almost always advisable to have an attorney help you resolve your claim. If there is no "at-fault" driver, or if you were involved in a motor vehicle accident and you are not receiving your own PIP benefits, you may need to hire an attorney to represent you. If you have been seriously injured, or suffered a serious permanent disfigurement to your body, I advise you to consult with a motor vehicle accident attorney to make sure you are receiving all of the personal injury protection benefits you are entitled to receive under Michigan's No-Fault law.

A person involved in a motor vehicle accident caused by someone else's negligence who has suffered a serious impairment of a body function or serious permanent disfigurement should get legal advice as to their options for recovery and benefits that they may be entitled to under Michigan's No-Fault law. If contacted by a person purportedly representing the insurance company of the at-fault driver who caused your injuries, *it may not be in your best interests to settle your case for the at-fault driver's maximum insurance coverage.* There may be other options to explore that will be precluded if you settle your case by signing a release form for the at-fault driver's insurance company. There may be underinsurance benefits available from your own motor vehicle insurance carrier. A third party defendant's liability could be extinguished from a possible dram shop case or another insurance carrier's coverage could be lost by an individual settling on their own with an at-fault driver's motor vehicle insurance carrier.

TIP:

In 1999 the insurance industry performed a study to find out if people who had accident claims received more money from settlements by using an attorney than those who settled on their own. The study was performed by the Insurance Research Council (IRC), a non-profit organization that is supported by leading property and casualty insurance companies across the United States. *The IRC found that people who used an attorney received, on average, three and one-half times more money from settlements than those individuals who settled on their own.*

Each motor vehicle accident is fact-specific and the injuries to you and the available insurance coverage from one or more possible insurance carriers will be different in each case. Making sure that all of your options have been explored is very important as you will only have one opportunity to properly resolve compensation issues affecting your case.

Furthermore, determining who was at-fault in your motor vehicle accident may be complicated. As discussed in Chapter II a motor vehicle accident attorney may make a tremendous difference in determining who was at-fault. Sometimes the question of who was across the center line, or who went through the intersection on a yellow or red light may be at issue. Hiring an attorney to retain experts can make a tremendous difference in these types of cases. Ask an experienced motor vehicle accident attorney to review your case if you have had serious injuries, even if the police may have labeled the other driver not to have been at-fault. Again, in this author's opinion, it is always advisable to have a second opinion rendered if there is any question as to who was at-fault in causing a motor vehicle accident that caused your injuries.

Question: How much will it cost to hire an attorney?

Answer: Michigan personal injury attorneys who handle motor vehicle accidents typically do so by entering into a contingency fee agreement with you or the personal representative of the estate of a loved one who has died as a result of a motor vehicle accident. Such contingency fee agreements provide, by Michigan court rule, that the attorney fee is paid by receiving a percentage of the net proceeds recovered on behalf of you or your loved one's estate after payment of any expenses.

In almost all personal injury cases, your attorney will be paid by keeping a percentage or a portion of the final settlement or court award compensating you for your injury or for your loss of a loved one. The percentage will be discussed with you by the attorney you retain, and will be the subject of the contingency fee agreement. Contract law requires, for your protection, a written agreement which specifies the fee the lawyer or his law firm will charge so that there will be no misunderstanding about how much your case will cost. Most contingency fee agreements provide that you do not have to pay your lawyer for his or her services unless, and until, the case is settled or is resolved by a settlement or court verdict in your favor.

The agreement will stipulate that your attorney will work diligently on your case in exchange for receiving the percentage or portion of your settlement or court award outlined in the agreement. *The law requires that you be responsible for actual out-of-pocket costs, expenses incurred in any litigation, and attorney fees, unless the attorney fees are to be paid pursuant to a contingency fee agreement.* This is true even if the case is not settled or won. Most law firms, however, do not bill a client for any out-of-pocket expenses if the case does not result in a settlement or a favorable court award.

Almost all personal injury clients retain their attorney pursuant to a 33⅓ percent contingency fee agreement. Most injured parties simply cannot afford to advance to the attorney the sums necessary to pay for the costs of litigation (to retain experts, etc.) and to fairly compensate the attorney for his or her time on an hourly basis. The 33⅓ percent contingency fee has been arrived at based on numerous studies indicating that if a reasonable hourly rate were charged by a trial attorney experienced in handling personal injury claims, the contingency fee earned would typically equate to about the same legal expense for the injured party. The attorney also carries the risk that there will not be a favorable settlement and he or she will not be paid.

Question: A loved one died in a motor vehicle accident that may have been caused by someone else's negligence. Do I need an attorney to help me to pursue any possible claim I might have for the wrongful death of a loved one?

Answer: In a death case it almost always makes sense to hire a motor vehicle accident attorney to deal with the myriad issues that must be dealt with in order to resolve any claim for the wrongful death of a loved one.

Question: Which attorney should I hire to help me receive the benefits I am entitled to receive under Michigan's No-Fault law?

Answer: Trusting your personal injury case to an unknown attorney does not make sense. Seek out an experienced personal injury attorney who you know and trust or one recommended by individuals you know and trust.

I'm often asked "How do I know who to hire to help me through the legal hurdles to settle my loved one's case?" As discussed earlier, almost all experienced personal injury attorneys who handle motor vehicle cases charge the same legal fee pursuant to a one-third contingency agreement. So, if the legal fee will likely be the same, how do you know who is best suited to represent you and your loved one's estate? In answering this question, I tell people to ask around for recommendations. Here are some other things to think about in the decision process:

- In cases involving serious injuries to you or serious injuries to a loved one, you and/or the loved one will need to meet often with the attorney you select.
- Typically, an attorney who is experienced with the local courts where the matter may have to be litigated will be in the best position to assess the value of your claim should the matter have to be litigated.
- You should attempt to learn the motor vehicle accident attorney's track record for actually trying cases in the area where the accident occurred. The attorney, who knows local jurors and judges and the things that local judges and jurors value, is especially important to an insurance adjuster who has been

assigned to settle your case. Will the attorney you select be one who settles for whatever the insurance adjuster is willing to offer? Will the attorney selected by you be the type of attorney who tells the insurance adjuster what he or she believes your case is worth? Will the attorney be willing to try the case before a jury of your peers?

- Ask others whether the motor vehicle accident attorney you are considering retaining actually tries cases before juries and wins his cases. This will be the single biggest factor in determining whether the insurance company will be willing to pay the maximum dollar to settle your case. The concern of being hit with a "big jury verdict" is what drives most business decisions from the insurance company's point of view when deciding how much to pay to settle a case.

TIP:

You can also check out ratings of the attorneys being considered on the internet from third party sources such as AVVO and Martindale-Hubbell. Also check for testimonials from other individuals who have used the particular attorney you are considering. Most importantly, see how other local sources may have rated your possible choice. The "local factor" is especially important to insurance companies when they evaluate who they will have to deal with before a local jury if they cannot adjust your claim. Since over 90% of all personal injury claims are settled without actually going to trial, maximizing the settlement value of your case by selecting an experienced local motor vehicle accident attorney the insurance company respects is extremely important.

If your case will be tried before a central or northern Michigan jury, it usually doesn't make sense to hire an attorney from Detroit or Southfield. Conversely, if you were injured in Detroit or southeast Michigan, and you live in the Detroit area, then it usually wouldn't make sense to hire an attorney from central or northern Michigan. Sometimes, however, when a person lives in central or northern Michigan and is injured down state or even outside of Michigan, it may make sense to have an experienced local motor vehicle accident attorney help you settle your case. If litigation becomes necessary, your local attorney can retain local counsel or appear *pro hac vice* in another state to help litigate your case if a lawsuit has to be filed.

TIP:

Most people don't want to risk going to trial to have a jury determine the value of their case. **Having the option, however, to go to trial and have a jury of your peers decide whether the compensation being offered by the insurance company is a fair amount, keeps the insurance company from low-balling their settlement offer to you.** When the insurance company knows that you have selected a respected trial attorney, who is experienced in the court room, who knows what local judges and jurors typically look for, and is not afraid to try cases, then the settlement value of your case goes up dramatically!

Question: What if I am trying to decide who to hire to represent me in seeking compensation for the death of a person I loved?

Answer: As in the previous answer, there are several factors that need to be considered. If the accident was caused by the negligence of another driver, or if there is a question as to whether the accident was caused by another driver, then the following factors should be kept in mind:

- The attorney selected will have to file estate documents in the county where the deceased lived at the time of his/her death.
- You will need to visit frequently with the attorney to discuss legal and factual issues affecting your deceased loved one's case. Accordingly, traveling a great distance to meet with your legal counsel will affect you and other family members, as well.
- The attorney you select will provide you and other family members with personal advice regarding grief counselors available in your area to help each of you deal with the emotional loss of your loved one's death. When a young child dies, mothers and fathers generally grieve differently. Men tend to be more stoic, while women tend to be more open with their emotions and displaying their grief. Each person grieves differently. There are no generalizations that cover all situations. Nevertheless, having both the husband and the wife understand how the other spouse has to grieve is very important to lessening the stress between parents as they both suffer their individual loss.

The worst thing that can happen in the death of a minor child is for the death to drive a wedge between the deceased's child's parents leading to a divorce. Sadly, this happens in a high percentage of cases. A responsible local motor vehicle accident attorney will put the parents in touch with an experienced grief counselor.

- When a spouse has died, especially when minor children are involved, hiring an experienced local trial attorney who has successfully tried cases to verdict can be extremely important to obtaining financial compensation for family members. Referring to the personal track record of a local attorney for actually trying and winning cases in the area where the accident occurred and/or where the decedent lived at the time of the death can be critical to maximizing the recovery for family members. Family members entitled to assert a wrongful death claim include a spouse, children, children of a spouse, parents, siblings and grandparents left behind.

Chapter 5

Seven Mistakes That Can Harm Your Motor Vehicle Accident Claim

1. *Talking to an insurance company's adjuster before you have consulted with a motor vehicle accident attorney.*

   Many a claim is harmed when an injured party makes innocent statements that are later misconstrued as admissions against interest by the insurance company. It is always wise to talk to a motor vehicle accident attorney before giving statements to an insurance adjuster or an insurance company's investigator.

2. *Discussing your motor vehicle accident on social media sites.*

   Many cases have been seriously damaged by photos and statements posted on Facebook®, YouTube®, and other social media websites. Talking about your motor vehicle accident; how it happened; what you were doing before, during, or after the accident, can seriously undermine your case. Posting your progress of getting better, especially if you are overly optimistic, can be used against you as "Exhibit 1" in your case. Refrain from discussing how your motor vehicle accident happened, and how you are recovering from your injuries. Anything can and will be used against you by the insurance adjuster to point out why your case should be valued lower than you are requesting. Whatever you say or do that ends up on the Internet can undermine the value of your case.

3. *Hiding past accidents from your attorney.*

Once you begin a case, the other side will be interested in knowing how many past accidents you have been involved in where you have been injured. The reality is that they probably already know the answers to the question as they have easy access to such information. All insurance companies subscribe to insurance databases and often the only reason they ask you this question at a deposition is to find out if you are being truthful.

If you have been involved in other motor vehicle accidents, your attorney can investigate this and make a determination as to whether this is an issue for you and your case. If you do not advise your attorney, however, about your prior accidents and misrepresent your accident history to your own attorney or to the insurance company, such misrepresentation will almost guarantee your case being torpedoed.

I have had former clients advise us that they didn't need to disclose their prior accidents because it didn't matter. This is not a good answer. The insurance company will likely know whether you have been involved in a prior accident. If you withhold such information from your lawyer or the insurance company, such dishonesty will usually end up harming your case.

4. Hiding other injuries.

It goes without saying that you should be upfront and honest with your attorney about any injuries that have occurred before or after this accident, whether from a motor vehicle accident or from some other accident. Again, if you saw a doctor or other health care provider, there likely is a record in existence that the insurance company will learn about. Your attorney can explain prior health issues by showing how your current accident has aggravated a pre-existing condition that you had if your attorney knows about it. If you are not honest with your own attorney, and lie about it, try to cover up a prior health issue, and the insurance company finds out, your case may be torpedoed. Remember there is very little privacy in America today. When you make an insurance claim your life becomes an open book regarding your past medical history.

If you are dishonest with your attorney about your prior medical histories, that can be a basis for your attorney terminating his or her client relationship with you. If it is determined that you have deliberately misled your attorney, such dishonesty typically results in your attorney discharging you as his or her client. Having said that, I find that this rarely happens with our clients. Nevertheless, it is important to advise you about how such a mistake can sink your No-Fault insurance claim.

5. Do not have a lawyer steer you to a medical doctor or chiropractor that the lawyer uses all the time.

If a lawyer has one doctor or chiropractor to whom he refers all of his motor vehicle accident cases, this fact will, typically come out during litigation. While the client may not know how many of that lawyers other clients have been referred in the past five years to a particular doctor or chiropractor, you can rest assured that the insurance company will notice or find out about it during discovery. This will cause credibility issues when the doctor or chiropractor testifies. The jury will certainly hear about the fact that he has treated over one hundred patients referred to him from the same lawyer over the last five years. There are exceptions to this concern. It is perfectly legitimate for your attorney to suggest or recommend a specialist. If every client, however, is being referred to the same medical doctor or chiropractor this can become a huge problem. Accordingly, beware of the attorney who has a stack of doctor or chiropractor cards in his or her office. You need to ask the right questions and fully understand the business relationship, if any, between the attorney and the doctor or chiropractor to whom he may be referring you.

6. *Not having accurate tax returns.*

In most cases, a claimant will have lost income because of a motor vehicle accident. In most cases, you will only be able to claim such lost income if your past tax returns have been honestly filed. You may risk going to jail by claiming a loss of income which was not properly reported on past income tax returns. Again, being honest with your attorney is the only way to proceed because your attorney can only deal with a problem if your attorney knows about "the problem."

Be aware that you will most certainly be required to produce your tax returns if you file a law suit and claim a loss of wages. If you are dishonest and do not file honest tax returns, this will come back to haunt you in your injury case. If you have not claimed income on your past tax returns, your loss of earnings income will usually be limited to that previously reported on tax returns.

7. Misrepresenting your activity level.

Insurance companies routinely hire private investigators to conduct videotaped surveillance. If you claim you cannot run, climb, or stoop, and you are observed and recorded "breakdancing," you can forget about your claim. If you have a debilitating leg injury or back injury, you should not be recorded building a new deck on the back of your house or removing leaves from your eaves.

Chapter 6

Frequently Asked Questions Regarding Michigan's No-Fault Law

Question: If I'm injured in a motor vehicle accident how long do I have to file a claim for benefits?

Answer: If we're talking about benefits from your own insurance company, or the insurance company designated to provide your **personal injury protection (PIP)** benefits (wage loss, replacement services, reimbursement for medical-related expenses, etc.), then you have one year from the time you are eligible to receive such benefits.

Whenever an injury prevents you from working, you are entitled to wage loss benefits up to a statutory maximum, for up to three years after the date of the motor vehicle accident. You are also entitled to $20 per day as reimbursement for replacement services for up to three years after the date of your accident. You are entitled to receive reimbursement for medical expenses, reasonably and necessarily incurred, for life. **That being said, however, if the claim for reimbursement is not made and/or paid one year from the date the medical-related expense was incurred, you will be denied recovery.** Don't wait until the one year period is about to expire, as you might need to consult with an attorney and give the attorney enough time to initiate a lawsuit to prevent losing a benefit you would otherwise be entitled to receive.

The period of time for instituting **a claim against an at-fault driver** is **three years from the date of the accident.** If a lawsuit has not been filed to recover for your injuries before the three year statute of limitation has expired, your claim will become time-barred and no recovery will be able to be made on your behalf. If a person died as a result of a motor vehicle accident and the cause for the person's death was the negligence of another at-fault driver, the three year general period of limitation may be extended. If a person dies before or within 30 days of when the statute of limitations has run, the personal representative may file an action within two years after Letters of Authority have been issued, even though the period of limitation has passed. However, an action under this provision must be brought within three years after the period of limitation has passed.

Question: How much am I entitled to receive if I am injured and cannot work?

Answer: Typically, the insurance company responsible for paying your wage loss benefits will offer to pay you 85% of the gross wages you were earning at the time of being injured in a motor vehicle accident. The 85% figure is not taxable to you, and for many people, this is a better deal for them since their tax rate for federal and state taxes typically exceeds 15% of their gross wages. There are some individuals, however, who might be employed on a part-time basis earning minimum wage, where even the 15% figure would be high. If you are earning less than $15,000 per year, your taxable rate could be less than 10%. Most insurance companies will still typically offer you 85% of your gross wages because it's what they're used to paying. Check with an accountant to see if you might be able to negotiate obtaining 90% of your gross wages. The law simply states that the insurance company may deduct *up to* 15% based on the tax rate that is applied to your gross wages.

Question: What are replacement services?

Answer: Personal Injury Protection benefits require that the insurance company reimburse the injured party, or members of the family of a deceased party for hired services that could have been performed by the injured party or the deceased for up to three years after the time of the accident.

Michigan's No-Fault Act caps this reimbursement payment at $20 per day, seven days a week, for three years. Often, family members are the individuals who provide these types of services. Such services include household cleaning, laundry services, lawn care services, grocery shopping, snow shoveling, childcare functions, making vehicle repairs, preparing meals, and bathing family members. See Chapter II: Personal Injury Protection Benefits.

Question: If I am injured and cannot ambulate, can I receive benefits allowing me to have a different type of vehicle or to improve my living quarters?

Answer: Yes. In Michigan, our No-Fault law provides that the insurance company providing Personal Injury Protection benefits is also required to make home modifications and motor vehicle modifications to allow you to function properly, and potentially, to return to work. Home modifications include constructing ramps, widening doors, lowering countertops, installing elevators, etc. Vehicle modification, so that the individual can get in and out of their motor vehicle, are also reimbursable when necessary to enable an accident victim to drive the motor vehicle despite their accident-related limitations.

Question: Are chiropractic visits and/or physical therapy visits covered under No-Fault benefits?

Answer: Yes. Reasonable medical expenses include physical therapy and chiropractic care, as well as speech therapy, psychotherapy, vocational rehabilitation, counseling, job training, and job placement services.

Question: If I need someone to come into my home and take care of me, is this a benefit provided under Michigan's No-Fault Act?

Answer: Yes. In-home attendant care services can be provided to an injured party by outside agencies, a nurse, or a family member. Attendant care services may involve bathing, dressing, administering medicine, helping individuals use the toilet, and just monitoring the individual, including during periods of rest. *Attendant care services are in addition to replacement services*, and should not be confused with the $20 per day cap for hiring others to perform services that the injured party or deceased party previously was able to perform themselves.

Question: If my injuries cause me a lot of pain, is there something I can recover under Michigan's No-Fault Act?

Answer: Yes. In order to recover for your pain and suffering, mental anguish, depression, anxiety, embarrassment, and humiliation, as a result your injury, your injuries must be deemed to be a serious impairment of a body function.

This is what is known as "having a threshold injury." Body functions include the ability to walk, talk, sleep, think, hear, taste, smell, and function in the work place.

Additionally, the law allows you to recover for your embarrassment and mortification as a result of receiving serious and permanent scarring to your body. Both of these types of injuries, for your pain and suffering, and embarrassment for scarring, are referred to as non-economic damages. They are only able to be recovered if there is an at-fault driver who caused the impairment of one of your body functions or caused your permanent, serious scarring.

Question: Do I need an attorney to represent me in order to obtain the benefits I am entitled to under Michigan's No-Fault Act?

Answer: That depends. Typically, if you are attempting to receive Personal Injury Protection benefits the answer is, generally, no. Usually, the insurance company will provide you with the forms necessary to make your claim and you will be able to obtain the benefits you are entitled to receive under Michigan's No-Fault Act. There are times, however, for whatever reason, that you and the insurance company do not agree on the amount of money you should receive for wage loss, replacement services, or reimbursement for medical-related expenses. If you have significant injuries and/or require long-term care, it is wise to contact an attorney and discuss the wisdom of hiring a case manager to assist you in negotiating the benefits you are entitled to receive with the insurance company responsible for paying your PIP benefits.

When it comes to holding an at-fault driver responsible for economic losses that have been sustained or will be sustained in excess of your Personal Injury Protection coverage, then it makes sense to hire an attorney to help you recover the compensation that may be available to you. If you have received a serious injury impairing one of your body functions or a serious permanent disfigurement then it also makes sense to consult with a motor vehicle injury attorney to pursue additional compensation available from an at-fault driver. Without the assistance of an experienced motor vehicle accident attorney, it is unlikely that you will receive all of the benefits you could be entitled to receive from what is known as a third party claim against an at-fault driver.

In the case of the death of a loved one who died as a result of a motor vehicle accident caused by someone else's negligence, it is almost always required that you receive assistance from an experienced motor vehicle accident attorney to maximize the recovery for the next-of-kin of the decedent. There are myriad issues involved in pursuing a wrongful death action and you will need help from an experienced motor vehicle accident attorney to maximize the estate's recovery.

Chapter 7

Why Hiring a Local Accident Attorney Might Be a Smart Move

Throughout this book, I have stressed the importance of hiring different types of experts to maximize the recovery for you or the estate of a loved one for a first or third party motor vehicle claim. Whether it be a biomechanical, accident reconstruction, conspicuity, or vocational expert, employing the right expert to quickly preserve and analyze evidence can make all the difference in the world when it comes to proving what did or did not happen in your motor vehicle case.

When a motor vehicle accident caused the death of a loved one, generally grieving family members are left behind to sort out the "Why?" and "What do we do now?" questions. A *probate estate* must be opened in probate court so a personal representative can be appointed to represent the next-of-kin to pursue any claim the estate and/or the next-of-kin may have as a result of the wrongful death of a loved one.

All of the above tasks are usually much easier if an experienced, local motor vehicle accident law firm is employed to assist the parties. If the motor accident occurred in Central or Northern Michigan that is where the claim will have to be tried in court if the parties are not able to reach a settlement with the insurance company representing the at-fault driver. Hiring a local law firm experienced in litigating motor vehicle accident claims can make all the difference in maximizing the recovery for the claimants.

Knowing how local juries value claims, and what factors are more important to a Central or Northern Michigan juror, as opposed to a Southfield, Detroit, or Grand Rapids juror, can be very important. Detroit jurors live in a different social environment than those who live in Isabella County, Gratiot County, Midland County, Clare County, Gladwin County, Roscommon County, etc. What is taken for granted as acceptable behavior in one locale, as opposed to another, can be strikingly different. Hunting deer and fishing for the elusive trout is a much more serious "business" in Central and Northern Michigan than in Southfield, Michigan.

Knowing the differences in the attitudes of jurors and how local judges and their court staff operate, can substantially affect the outcome of your case. Knowing what works in

Central and Northern Michigan, as opposed to what works in Detroit, is very important to obtaining the best possible results for you and for maximizing your claim.

When it comes to a death case, an attorney who knows local grief counselors and local law enforcement agencies can make a big difference to the decedent's next-of-kin. Often, when a death has been caused by an at-fault driver, criminal charges may be part of the aftermath. Having a local attorney familiar with the players who will be involved with investigating and potentially prosecuting the at-fault driver can be very helpful. The local attorney may have a working relationship with the police agency involved in the investigation. When it comes to prosecutors and judges representing the public's interest in the case, local relationships can be important to the next-of-kin. Explaining the rights of victims to address the court at sentencing, and to have input into plea negotiations to resolve the case is usually comforting to grieving family members. Experienced, local attorneys usually know all the local players involved in the process. This knowledge allows local counsel to better predict the outcome of certain procedural steps that will likely occur along the way to resolving any criminal charges.

Typically, a local motor vehicle accident attorney will personally know the county medical examiner who will, in all likelihood, have signed the decedent's death certificate, and also possibly the pathologist who actually performed the autopsy. Based on previous depositions of such individuals and established relationships, a local experienced motor vehicle attorney may have easy access to such individuals by way of a phone call. That type of access allows the local attorney to quickly obtain detailed information on the decedent that may be relevant to the estate's claim for compensation for any conscious pain and suffering incurred by the decedent after being injured but before death.

Accordingly, when it comes to settling motor vehicle accident claims, it usually makes the most sense to hire an experienced motor vehicle accident attorney from a local law firm located near you, near where the decedent lived, or near where the accident occurred. The local factor also plays a huge role in the insurance company's decision regarding how much they may be willing to pay to adjust the claim rather than take a chance with a jury verdict. Insurance adjusters are usually familiar with local attorneys who are respected in the area where the case has to be adjusted or may have to be tried in court.

I hope by now you have learned about your **first party** rights to personal insurance protection (PIP) benefits from your own insurance company or the insurance carrier responsible to pay such PIP benefits pursuant to our State's priority rules. I also hope you have an understanding of your rights to pursue a **third party** claim against an at-fault party who caused the motor vehicle accident. And lastly, I hope that this book has given you an idea of how we do things at Barberi Law to best serve our clients.

I can attest that at our law firm, every case we take, we take personally. This phrase is not a slogan, rather it describes how we act when representing our clients. Every member of our staff works very hard to obtain the best possible outcome for each of our individual clients for their particular case.

If you trust us with your case, you can rest assured that our legal team will do our collective best to serve you and your needs throughout our representation of you. In every motor vehicle accident case, a minimum of two attorneys and one paralegal are assigned to work on your case to make sure someone is always available to answer your questions and just to be there for you and your family as we process your claim to a favorable settlement, or if necessary, to a trial or verdict.

About the Author

Joseph Barberi has been practicing law in the Central Michigan area for over thirty years. Prior to entering private practice, Mr. Barberi served as the elected Prosecuting Attorney for Isabella County for 12 years. During his tenure as Prosecuting Attorney, he was also elected by his peers to serve as President of the Prosecuting Attorney's Association of Michigan. By virtue of this position, being President of PAAM, Mr. Barberi worked with Michigan's Attorney General and Governor on a regular basis concerning criminal justice issues, some of which involved enforcement of Michigan's Motor Vehicle Code.

Mr. Barberi has tried over 300 jury trials and won all but three. Mr. Barberi holds Isabella County's record for the largest single jury verdict in a motor vehicle accident case. Mr. Barberi recently settled a Mid–Michigan motor vehicle death case for 1.35 million dollars without filing a lawsuit. Mr. Barberi employs jury consultants both before and during litigation, and has, on several occasions, conducted and participated in mock jury trials during litigation to ascertain the likely maximum jury value of a particular case.

Mr. Barberi is a member of Michigan's Association of Justice, and has also lectured at Michigan Association of Justice seminars. Most recently, Mr. Barberi addressed members of the Michigan Association of Justice regarding the use of digital motion x-ray (DMX) to document ligamentous and tendon injuries sustained by individuals during motor vehicle accidents.

Mr. Barberi is also a well-known trial attorney in other areas of the law. In addition to handling motor vehicle accident cases, including truck accidents and motorcycle accidents, Mr. Barberi also handles medical malpractice claims, serious dog bite cases, and premises liability claims.

IMPORTANT DISCLAIMER

This is an informational consumer guide intended to assist the public. It is not legal advice. It is not a substitute for informed professional legal, psychiatric, psychological, tax, investment, accounting, counseling, or other professional advice. Laws change, court decisions interpreting and changing case precedent occur weekly; all of these changes can cause advice to change as well, even advice based on the same facts.

Some observant readers may come across a fact or two that might appear to be in error. They may consider writing me to point out such observations. In our world, my advice is we should all try to save trees (paper). There are mistakes in this book, as with most books. No matter how hard one tries to avoid mistakes—mistakes will always occur. My hope is that such unintended error will be insignificant in nature, and that those observant readers finding error will be both understanding and forgiving.

Accordingly, comments and opinions set forth in this book should not be relied on as legal advice, or professional advice of any other kind. Reading this book does not create an attorney/client relationship between the author and the reader. In order to receive proper legal advice or professional advice of any kind, an individual needs to discuss his or her unique facts with a professional who will then be in a position to give the client or patient, their best professional advice.

How to Subscribe to Our Newsletter or Get it Sent to a Friend or Family Member

If you are reading this book, you might also be receiving our monthly hardcopy newsletter which covers interesting stories about the law, news items that we believe you will find very useful and interesting, and other information to keep you up-to-date on relevant changes to Michigan's laws.

If you would like to recommend family and/or friends who you believe might also be interested in receiving our newsletter, simply provide us with their names and addresses. We would be delighted to reach more interested individuals. We'll send each of them our monthly newsletter, along with a note telling them that you graciously referred them. Don't worry, we don't spam nor do we share information with any other parties! (If, for any reason, they don't want to receive it, there is always a toll-free number that can be called to remove a name from the subscription list.)

If you are not receiving our newsletter and would like to, we'll be happy to sign you up for a free subscription.

Subscribing Is Easy

Call with names and addresses (and email addresses if available), or send requests via fax, the form at the bottom of our site, or standard mail.

Call: 989-773-3423 **Online:** barberilawfirm.com
Fax 989-772-6444 **Mail:** BARBERI LAW
2305 Hawthorn Drive, Ste. C,
Mt. Pleasant, MI 48858.

★We also have an email version of the newsletter, and if you would prefer to receive your copy in your inbox, simply provide us with your email address.

We Appreciate Your Referrals
Thank You for Your Trust and Confidence

How to Get another Copy of This Book

If others want a free copy of this book, or you want an additional copy to give to a friend, fill out the form below and mail it to us, or simply send us a note with the names and addresses of the people you think would appreciate a free copy. We will promptly put one in the mail.

*We also have an e-book version that we can send via email.

If confidentiality is an issue, you can pick up a copy from our law offices:

BARBERI LAW

2305 Hawthorn Drive, Suite C,

Mt. Pleasant, MI 48858

Copies can also be ordered at Amazon.com, *but there is a $18.95 sales price*!

--✂

Yes, please send me a free copy of Mr. Barberi's

THE MICHIGAN MOTOR VEHICLE ACCIDENT BOOK

Name: _____

Address: _____

City: _____ State: _____ Zip: _____

Email address: _____

☐ Please check this box if you would like the e-book version.

We Appreciate Your Referrals Thank You for Your Trust and Confidence

BARBERI LAW

EVERY CASE WE TAKE,
WE TAKE PERSONALLY.℠

2305 Hawthorn Drive, Ste C,
Mt. Pleasant, MI 48858

1-800-336-3423

www.barberilawfirm.com

WA